Read Real NIHONGO

JN090761

Customs of Japan
ニッポンのしきたり

Tsuchiya Haruhito
土屋晴仁

Ginny Tapley Takemori ＝ translator
竹森ジニー＝訳

IBCパブリッシング

装　幀＝見増　勇介、関屋　晶子(ym design)
イラスト＝目黒久美子、テッド高橋
翻訳協力＝ Matt Treyvaud

本書は2017年に弊社から刊行されたFurigana JAPAN『ニッポンのしきたり』(土屋晴仁著、竹森ジニー訳)を
再編集し、改訂したものです。

About the *Read Real NIHONGO* Series

Reading Sets You Free

The difficulty of reading Japanese is perhaps the greatest obstacle to the speedy mastery of the language. A highly motivated English speaker who wants to make rapid progress in a major European language such as Spanish, French or German need only acquire a grasp of the grammar and a smattering of vocabulary to become able to at least attempt to read a book. Thanks to a common alphabet, they can instantly identify every word on the page, locate them in a dictionary, and figure out—more or less—what is going on.

With Japanese, however, *kanji* ideograms make it infinitely harder to make the jump from reading with guidance from a teacher to reading freely by oneself. The chasm dividing the short example sentences of textbooks from the more intellectually rewarding world of real-world books and articles can appear unbridgeable. Japanese—to borrow Nassim Taleb's phrase—is an "Extremistan" language. *Either* you master two thousand *kanji* characters with their various readings to achieve breakthrough reading proficiency and the capacity for self-study *or* you fail to memorize enough *kanji*, your morale collapses, and you retire, tired of floating in a limbo of semi-literacy. At a certain point, Japanese is all or nothing, win or lose, put up or shut up.

The benefits of staying the course and acquiring the ability to read independently are, of course, enormous.

Firstly, acquiring the ability to study by yourself without needing a teacher increases the absolute number of hours that you can study from "classroom time only" to "as long as you want." If there is any truth to the theories about 10,000 hours of practice being needed to master any skill, then clearly the ability to log more hours of Japanese self-study has got to be a major competitive advantage.

Secondly, exposure to longer texts means that your Japanese input rises in simple quantitative terms. More Japanese *going into* your head means that, necessarily, more Japanese *stays in* your head! As well as retaining more words and idioms, you will also start to develop greater mental stamina. You will get accustomed to digesting Japanese in real-life "adult" portions rather than the child-sized portions you were used to in the classroom.

Thirdly, reading will help you develop tolerance for complexity as you start using context to help you figure things out for yourself. When reading a book, the process goes something like this: You read a sentence; should you fail to understand it first time, you read it again. Should it still not make sense to you, you can go onto the next sentence and use the meaning of that one to "reverse-engineer" the meaning of its predecessor, and so on. By doing this, you will become self-reliant, pragmatic and—this is significant—able to put up with gaps in your understanding without panicking, because you know they are only temporary. You will morph into a woodsman of language, able to live off the land, however it may be.

That is the main purpose of the *Read Real NIHONGO* series: to propel you across the chasm that separates those who read Japanese from those who cannot.

Furigana the Equalizer

Bilingual books have been popular in Japan since the 1990s. Over time, they have grown more sophisticated, adding features like comprehensive page-by-page glossaries, illustrations and online audio. What makes the *Read Real NIHONGO* series—a relative latecomer to the scene—special?

It all comes down to *furigana*. This is the first ever series of bilingual books to include *furigana* superscript above every single *kanji* word in the text. Commonly used in children's books in Japan, *furigana* is a tried-and-tested, non-intrusive and efficient way to learn to read *kanji* ideograms. By enabling you to decipher every word immediately, *furigana* helps you grasp the meaning of whole passages faster without needing to get bogged down in fruitless and demoralizing searches for the pronunciation of individual words.

By providing you with the pronunciation, *furigana* also enables you to commit new words to memory right away (since we remember more by sound than by appearance), as well as giving you the wherewithal to look them up, should you want to go beyond the single usage example on the facing English page. *Read Real NIHONGO* provides a mini-glossary on each right page to help you identify and commit to memory the most important words and phrases.

Raw Materials for Conversation

So much for *furigana* and the language-learning aspect—now for the content. The books in this series are all about Japan, from its customs, traditions and cuisine to its history, politics and economy. Providing essential insights into what makes the Japanese and their society tick, every book can help you as you transition from ignorant outsider to informed insider. The information the books contain gives you a treasure trove of raw materials you can use in conversations with Japanese people. Whether you want to amaze your interlocutors with your knowledge of Japanese religion, impress your work colleagues with your mastery of party-seating etiquette and correct bowing angles, or enjoy a heated discussion of the relative merits of arranged marriages versus love marriages, *Read Real NIHONGO* is very much the gift that keeps on giving.

We are confident that this series will help everyone—from students to businesspeople and diplomats to tourists—start reading Japanese painlessly while also learning about Japanese culture. Enjoy!

Tom Christian
Editor-in-Chief
Read Real NIHONGO Series

はじめに

　18歳から東京で暮らしていた僕は、日々の暮らしの中で日本的な「しきたり」を実感することは少なかった。もちろん新年の「初詣で」や、結婚式や葬式も経験したが、ちょっとフォーマルなイベントに参加するという程度の感覚でしかなかった気がする。その認識や感覚が変化したのは、2005年に故郷の佐渡島（新潟県）に帰って暮らすようになってからだ。老いた両親に介護が必要になり、2年後には父を8年後には母を看取った。

　田舎には古い伝統や慣習が残り、良くも悪くも人々の繋がりが濃密だ。そこでの祭りや祝い事あるいは葬儀のやり方は何世代にもわたって受け継がれている。「なぜ、そうするのか」と考えさせられることも多かった。戸惑いより好奇心が大きかったが、調べたことや経験した、感じたことを「ニッポンのしきたり」という本にまとめる機会ができた。

　本書によって、海外のみなさんが、日本人が日々の暮らしの中で培ってきた習慣、マナー、知恵などを理解する一助になることを願っています。

土屋 晴仁

□日本的なしきたり　traditional Japanese customs
□初詣で　shrine visit at New Year
□認識　perception
□故郷　one's old home

□介護　care
□看取る　take care of the sick to death
□田舎　countryside
□慣習　customs

Preface

After moving to Tokyo at the age of eighteen, I never really experienced traditional Japanese customs in my daily life. Of course, I'd go on the customary shrine visit at New Year, and to weddings and funerals, but I only ever really felt like I was attending rather formal events. That all changed in 2005 when I moved back home to Sado Island (Niigata) in order to care for my aging parents. My father passed away two years later, and my mother eight years later.

Old traditions and customs are still alive in the countryside where, for better or for worse, there are strong bonds between people. The festivals, celebratory events, and funerals in these areas have been handed down through many generations. There were many things that made me wonder, "Why is it done that way?" I wasn't baffled so much as curious, and I was given the opportunity to summarize what I'd researched, experienced, and felt in the book *Customs of Japan*.

I hope that this book will help people overseas understand the customs, manner and folk wisdom that the Japanese have developed in the course of everyday life.

Haruhito Tsuchiya

□良くも悪くも for better of for worse
□濃密 dense
□受け継がれている be handed down
□戸惑い baffled

□培う develop

もくじ

はじめに ……………………………………………… 6

1 **年間行事** ……………………………………… 13
 1. お正月 ……… 14
 2. 節分 ……… 20
 3. お花見 ……… 24
 4. 節句 ……… 28
 5. お彼岸 ……… 34
 6. 夏の土用 ……… 36
 7. お盆 ……… 38
 8. お月見 ……… 40
 9. お祭り ……… 44
 10. 大晦日 ……… 46

2 **人生** …………………………………………… 51
 1. 出産 ……… 52
 2. 七五三 ……… 56
 3. 成人 ……… 58
 4. 賀寿 ……… 62
 5. 厄年 ……… 68

3 **婚礼・葬儀・宗教** ……………………… 71
 1. 婚約まで ……… 72
 2. 結婚式と披露宴 ……… 76

Contents

Preface ···7

1　**Events from Throughout the Year** ················13

　1. New Year *15*

　2. *Setsubun*: The End of Winter *21*

　3. *Ohanami*: Blossom Viewing *25*

　4. Seasonal Festivals *29*

　5. *Ohigan*: Equinoctial Weeks *35*

　6. *Doyō*: The Hottest Part of Summer *37*

　7. *Obon* *39*

　8. *Otsukimi*: Moon Viewing *41*

　9. *Omatsuri*: Festivals *45*

　10. *Ōmisoka*: New Year's Eve *47*

2　**Life Events**···*51*

　1. Birth *53*

　2. *Shichi-go-san*: Childhood Milestones *57*

　3. Coming of Age *59*

　4. Long-life Celebrations *63*

　5. *Yakudoshi*: Unlucky Years *69*

3　**Weddings, Funerals, and Religion** ···········*71*

　1. Courtship and Engagement *73*

　2. The Wedding Ceremony and Reception *77*

3. 式日／六曜 80

4. 葬儀 82

5. 神と仏 86

6. 民間信仰 92

4 つき合い ·· 101

1. お中元／お歳暮 102

2. 上座／下座 104

3. 宴会 106

4. あいさつ 110

5 衣・食・住 ·· 115

1. 着物・小物 116

2. 食品 122

3. 家 128

4. 暮らし方 134

6 その他 ·· 139

1. 年・月・時間 140

2. 縁起かつぎ 142

3. 図像 148

4. レジャー 152

5. 趣味 158

付録：イラストで見る日本の家 ······················ 162

3. Auspicious and Unlucky Days *81*

4. Funerals *83*

5. Gods and the Buddha *87*

6. Folk Beliefs *93*

4 Social Events ·············· *101*

1. Mid-year and Year-end Gifts *103*

2. Seating Etiquette *105*

3. *Enkai*: Parties *107*

4. *Aisatsu*: Greeting People *111*

5 Clothes, Food, and Homes ············· *115*

1. Kimonos and Accessories *117*

2. Food *123*

3. Homes *129*

4. Lifestyle *135*

6 Miscellaneous ······················· *139*

1. Dates and Times *141*

2. Attracting Luck *143*

3. Iconography *149*

4. Leisure *153*

5. Hobbies *159*

Bonus: **Illustrated guide to the Japanese house** ····· *162*

1

ねんかんぎょうじ
年間行事

Events from
Throughout the Year

1. お正月

01

新しい神様をお迎えする準備

　日本の神道では、正月になると福をもたらす神様が家々にやってくると考えられた。そこでそれぞれの家庭では神棚を飾り、家の中をきれいにし、玄関には目印となる松の飾り物（門松）を置いた。神棚の飾りで大事なのは榊の葉としめ縄を新しくすることで、そこが神様の寄り付く神聖な場所となる。神様への供え物としては大小の丸い餅を重ねた「鏡餅」が欠かせない。餅は米をついて作る伝統食品であり、豊穣のシンボルともされる。それを丸い形にして「鏡餅」と呼ぶのは、三種の神器の一つである「銅鏡」に見立てるからで、神棚以外にも「床の間」など家の中心となる神聖な場所にも置かれる。

　こうした準備は前年の12月28日までにすませておかねばならない。年末ぎりぎりになって飾り始めるのは縁起が悪いとされる。

正月の神棚の様子

Kamidana at New Year's

1. New Year

Preparing to welcome the new gods

According to Shinto belief, New Year is the time when the *kami*, or gods, bring good fortune to homes. To this end, families clean their houses, decorate their *kamidana* (altar to the gods), and place a *kadomatsu* pine decoration by the front entrance. The *kamidana* is decorated with fresh *sakaki* leaves and a new *shimenawa* rope to indicate the sacred space where the *kami* may approach. The *kagami mochi*, made with a small, round rice cake placed on top of a larger round rice cake, is an essential offering to the *kami*. *Mochi* rice cakes are a traditional food made from polished white rice, and also considered a symbol of a good harvest. The *kagami mochi*, literally "mirror *mochi*," is given its round shape and name after the bronze mirror that is one of the Three Sacred Treasures, and it can be placed on the *kamidana*, or in another sacred space at the heart of the home such the *tokonoma* alcove.

These preparations must be completed by December 28, and it is considered bad luck to leave the New Year decorations until the last minute.

☐ 福をもたらす bring good fortune
☐ 神棚 altar to the gods
☐ 玄関 front entrance
☐ 榊 Cleyera japonica
☐ 神聖な場所 sacred space
☐ 供え物 offering
☐ 餅 rice cake
☐ 伝統食品 traditional food
☐ 豊穣 good harvest
☐ 三種の神器 Three Sacred Treasures
☐ 銅鏡 bronze mirror
☐ 縁起が悪い bad luck

「元旦」には「初詣で」に行く

新しい年の最初の日、1月1日は「元旦」と呼ばれる。「元」ははじめ、「旦」は朝の意味である。元旦はその1年の計画を立てるべき日とされ、家族や近所の人とは「おめでとう」とあいさつを交わす。たくさんの「年賀状」も家々に配達されるが、最近は電子メールでの「おめでとう」メッセージ交換が盛んだ。

新年を迎えて何かの行動を起こす場合は、なんでも「初」の字が頭につく。近くの神社や寺にお参りに行くのは「初詣で」である。日の出の太陽も「初日の出」として尊ばれる。初めて見る夢は「初夢」で、縁起の良い夢が見られれば1年が幸せになる。

毎年変わる主役「年男」「年女」

新年を迎えてちょっとした注目を集める人がいる。その年の「干支」と生まれた年の「干支」が同じになる「年男」と「年女」だ。これは日本だけでなく、歴史的な中華文明圏(中国、韓国、日本、ベトナム、タイなど)に共通の陰陽五行思想に基づくもので、1年ごとに12種類の動物がシンボルになる。「子=鼠」「丑=牛」「寅=虎」「卯=兎」「辰=龍」「巳=蛇」「午=馬」「未=羊」「申=猿」「酉=鶏」「戌=犬」「亥=猪」の順で、12年ごとに自分の年がやってくることになる。

The first shine visit of the New Year

New Year's Day, January 1, is called 元旦 *gantan*, which is written with kanjis meaning "beginning" and "morning." *Gantan* is the day for making plans for the year, and for family members and neighbors to congratulate each other. Many New Year Cards are also delivered, and recently e-cards have become so popular.

All actions to greet the New Year are prefixed with the kanji 初, which means "first." The first visit to a shrine or temple is 初詣で (*hatsumōde*). The first sunrise is revered as 初日の出 (*hatsu hinode*). The first dream is 初夢 (*hatsuyume*), and if it is an auspicious dream the year to come will be a happy one.

- □ 元旦 New Year's Day
- □ あいさつを交わす congratulate each other
- □ 年賀状 New Year Card
- □ 盛ん popular
- □ ～の字が頭につく be prefixed with
- □ 神社 shrine
- □ 寺 temple
- □ 初詣で the first visit to a shrine or temple
- □ 初日の出 the first sunrise
- □ 尊ぶ revere
- □ 縁起の良い auspicious

Men and women born in the current year of the Oriental Zodiac

Certain people get a little extra attention every New Year. These are the *toshi-otoko* and *toshi-onna*, the men and women born in the current year of the traditional twelve-animal Oriental zodiac. This system is based on the doctrine of yin yang and the five elements, in which each year of a twelve-year cycle is symbolized by a different animal, and is followed not just in Japan, but also in other countries historically influenced by Chinese culture (China, Korea, Japan, Vietnam, Thailand, and others). The order is rat, ox, tiger, rabbit, dragon, snake, horse, sheep, monkey, rooster, dog, and boar.

- □ 歴史的な historically
- □ 動物 animal
- □ 鼠 rat
- □ 牛 ox
- □ 虎 tiger
- □ 兎 rabbit
- □ 龍 dragon
- □ 蛇 snake
- □ 馬 horse
- □ 羊 sheep
- □ 猿 monkey
- □ 鶏 rooster
- □ 犬 dog
- □ 猪 boar

正月に食べるのは「おせち料理」

元旦から3日ぐらいまでの間、食卓を飾るのは「おせち料理」である。えびや数の子、黒豆など縁起が良いとされる食材を使って保存できるように味付けし、重箱にきれいに盛り付けたものである。関東と関西では中身が異なるが、自宅で作るのは大変なので、近年では有名料理店ブランドのものが、デパートやコンビニやネット通販などで手に入る。ほかには、餅と魚や鶏肉などを入れた吸い物（雑煮）や薬草酒（お屠蘇）を用意するが、基本的に主婦は台所仕事はしなくてすむから大助かりだ。

「祝い肴」「口取り」「焼き物」「酢の物」「煮物」の5種類に分かれており、それぞれにおめでたい意味がある

Osechi ryōri is divided into five categories: "festive dishes," "appetizers," "grilled dishes," "vinegared dishes," and "simmered dishes," each with its own auspicious meaning.

子供たちは「お年玉」をもらう

お正月を一番楽しみにしているのは子供たちだろう。というのもこの時ばかりは遊んでいても叱られないし、親や親せきなど年長者から小遣いがもらえるからだ。古くは神様に供えた餅を分け与え、それには「魂」（たま＝玉）が宿っているとされたからだという説もある。

Osechi ryōri: special dishes prepared for New Year

The dishes that grace the dinner table for the first three days of the year are known as *osechi ryōri*. These are made from ingredients considered auspicious, such as prawns, herring roe, and black beans, that are seasoned and preserved, and arranged pleasingly in stacking boxes known as *jūbako*. The contents vary between eastern and western Japan, but it is a lot of work to make at home so these days people purchase sets made by famous food brands and sold in department stores, convenience stores and on the Internet. Housewives do prepare some other dishes such as *zōni*, a soup containing *mochi* rice cakes and fish or chicken, and *otoso,* sake infused with herbs, but on the whole they are saved the trouble of cooking during this period.

□食卓 dinner table

□飾る grace

□えび prawn

□数の子 herring roe

□黒豆 black bean

□食材 ingredient

□味付けする be seasoned

□中身 contents

□近年では these days

□魚 fish

□鶏肉 chicken

□基本的に on the whole

□主婦 housewife

Otoshidama: gifts of money to children at New Year

Children are probably the ones who most look forward to New Year. Not only is it the only time they can play without being scolded, but they also receive pocket money from the grown-ups, including their parents and relatives. There is a theory that this derives from the olden days when they would divide up the *mochi* offering that was prepared for the god, *tama* being a homophone for the words "soul" (魂) and "ball" (玉).

□子供たち children

□叱る scold

□親 parent

□親せき relative

□年長者 grown-up

□小遣い pocket money

□魂 soul

□説 theory

お年玉を入れるポチ袋

Decorative paper envelope for giving New Year's gifts

2.節分

02

豆をまいて「福は内、鬼は外」

　毎年2月の3日頃になると、日本各地で「節分」の行事が行われる。この日は「立春」（春が始まるという意味）の前日であり、「節分」は季節の分かれ目との意味になる。その行事というのは、寺社やそれぞれの家で、「福は内、鬼は外！」と掛け声をかけながら炒った豆をまくのである。掛け声は「福＝幸福は家の中に入れ、鬼＝邪気は外に出ろ」という意味で、豆は邪気にぶつけるツブテだから、後で芽が出ないように炒ってあるのだ。もともとは宮中で大晦日に行われていた「鬼はらい」の行事が民間に広まったものといわれる。また、人々はその豆を年齢の数だけ（あるいは1つ余計に）食べることで体内の邪気もはらう。

最近の流行は「恵方巻き」

　現代の日本で広く行われている年間行事や習慣、しきたりの多くは、たくましい商魂とそれをおもしろがる消費者が一緒に作り上げたものである。クリスマスケーキやバレンタインチョコなどはその代表格だが、節分にも「恵方巻き」という新種が登場している。これは、節分の日に7種の具材で作った太巻き寿司を、その年に縁起の良い方角に向かって、黙って食べると願いごとが叶うというもの。戦前から一部のすし屋や海苔屋が仕掛けたものの廃れて、1989年に関西の大手コンビニが本格的に売り出してから年々認知度が高まっているといわれる。

2. *Setsubun*: The End of Winter

Bean scattering: "Fortune in and demons out!"

On February 3, *setsubun* events are held all over Japan. This is the day before *risshun*, the first day of spring, and marks the change in the season. At shrines and temples as well as individual houses, people scatter roasted beans while chanting "Fortune in and demons out!" This is to attract happiness into the house and drive out evil spirits. Since the beans are thrown at the evil spirits, they are roasted to ensure they do not sprout later. The custom is said to have derived from an event to drive out demons held at the Imperial Court on New Year's Eve, which later spread amongst the populace. People also eat the same number of beans as their age (or sometimes one extra) to drive evil spirits out of their body.

☐ 日本各地 all over Japan
☐ 季節 season
☐ 寺社 shrines and temples
☐ 福 fortune
☐ 鬼 demon
☐ 掛け声をかける chant
☐ 炒った豆 roasted bean
☐ 邪気 evil spirit
☐ ツブテ stone
☐ 芽が出る sprout
☐ 宮中 Imperial Court
☐ 民間 populace
☐ 年齢 age

「福豆」と呼ばれる大豆をまく
Soy beans called *fukumame* ("fortune beams") are used.

Ehōmaki sushi rolls: a recent trend

Many of the annual events and customs celebrated around Japan these days have been created by enterprising commercial spirit with the help of their amused consumers. The prime examples are Christmas cakes and Valentines' chocolates, but another is the new type of sushi rolls eaten at *setsubun*, called *ehōmaki*. These are thick rolls made from seven ingredients, and are eaten in silence facing in that year's lucky direction and making a wish. This was apparently a gimmick created by some prewar sushi makers and *nori* seaweed stores that had gone out of fashion, but which has been making a comeback since a major convenience store in Kansai started promoting it in 1989.

☐ 年間行事 annual event
☐ 習慣 custom
☐ 商魂 commercial spirit
☐ 消費者 consumer
☐ 代表格 prime example
☐ 具材 ingredient
☐ 太巻き thick roll
☐ 方角 direction
☐ 戦前 prewar
☐ 海苔 *nori* seaweed
☐ 廃れる go out of fashion

本当は1年に24もある「節分」

　日本の気候は四季がはっきりしている。だから春の始まり（立春）もあれば、夏も秋も冬もそれぞれの区切りがある。四季はさらに6つずつの区切りがあるので合計で24もの「節分」があることになる。これを「二十四節気」と呼ぶ。昼と夜の時間が等しい春分、秋分とか、最も寒い「大寒」、暑いのが「大暑」、冬ごもりしていた虫が顔を出す「啓蟄」、大気が冷えて結露する「白露」など詩的な名前もついている。これは陰暦にもとづく農事の目安だった。それぞれに行事もあったはずだ。しかし立春前の「節分」行事だけが継承されてきたのは、冬を経て迎えた春こそが生命再生のスタートとして喜ばれたからかもしれない。

神社での豆まき風景

Bean scattering in Ikuta Shrine, Kobe
photo by Shadi HIJAZI (Shadih~enwiki at English Wikipedia)

In fact, there are twenty-four *setsubun* every year

Japan's climate has four distinct seasons. Therefore, while you have the start of spring, you also have junctures for summer, autumn, and winter. Each of the four seasons have six further divisions, which means you therefore have a total of twenty-four seasonal changes. Since *setsubun* means literally "change in season," this means there are twenty-four *setsubun*. These are collectively known as *nijūshi sekki* (twenty-four divisions of the solar year). In addition to the spring and autumn equinoxes, when the day and night are the same length, there is *daikan*, which is the coldest period of the year, *taisho*, which is the hottest period, and some with poetic names like *keichitsu*, or awakening of insects, which is when bugs emerge from hibernation, and *hakuro*, or white dew, which is when the air cools and condenses as dew. These were agricultural guidlines based on the lunar calendar. Each of them must have had its own events. However, the fact that the only *setsubun* celebrated now is the one marking the end of winter is probably due the joy felt at the end of winter and regeneration of life at the start of spring.

- □ 気候 climate
- □ 春 spring
- □ 立春 start of spring
- □ 夏 summer
- □ 秋 autumn
- □ 冬 winter
- □ 区切り juncture, division
- □ 春分 spring equinox
- □ 秋分 autumn equinox
- □ 冬ごもり hibernation
- □ 虫 insect
- □ 顔を出す emerge
- □ 結露する condense
- □ 白露 white dew
- □ 詩的な poetic
- □ 陰暦 lunar calendar
- □ 農事の目安 agricultural guidline
- □ 継承する succeed
- □ 生命再生 regeneration of life

3. お花見

03

「花は桜木、人は武士」

　寒い冬が過ぎてうららかな春がやってくると、人々の心も浮き立ってくる。とくに桜の花が咲きだすと、日本人は「お花見」に出かけたくなってうずうずする。これが中国人ならもう少し早く咲く梅や桃の花なのだろうが、日本人は桜を見に出かけることだけを「お花見」という。それほどまでに桜が大好きな国民である。15世紀(室町時代)に活躍した禅宗の高僧である一休宗純も、「花は桜木、人は武士、魚は鯛、小袖(の模様)はもみじ…」が、一番好ましいものだと言った。

　お花見は花を観賞するだけではない。気の合う人たちと、桜の木の下で酒を飲んだり、持ち寄ったご馳走を食べたり、歌ったりして楽しむことがお花見である。

権力者たちも奨励したお花見

　日本の歴史上、もっとも盛大に行われた「お花見」とされるのは、関白・豊臣秀吉が1598年に京都の醍醐寺で行った「醍醐の花見」だといわれる。公家や武士から庶民まで約3000人が参加して、宴会や仮装行列などのアトラクションを楽しんだ。江戸時代の将軍 徳川吉宗(1684–1751)は、隅田川の堤や飛鳥山(王子)、御殿山(品川)など江戸の各地に桜を植え、庶民の憩いの場を作った。

3. *Ohanami*: Blossom Viewing

"The cherry among flowers, the samurai among men"

When the cold winter passes and cheerful spring arrives, people's spirits rise too. Especially when the cherries bloom, which is when Japanese people itch to attend *ohanami*, or blossom viewing parties. The Chinese may prefer the earlier plum and peach blossoms, but for the Japanese blossom viewing can only refer to cherry blossoms. This is how much we as a nation love them. The fifteenth century Zen Buddhist priest Ikkyū Sōjun also said that for him the most agreeable things were, "The cherry among flowers; the samurai among men; the sea bream among fish; the maple leaf among kimono patterns..."

Ohanami is not just about viewing blossoms. It is about enjoying time with friends and colleagues drinking sake, eating picnic fare, and singing songs beneath the blossoms.

☐ うららかな cheerful
☐ 浮き立つ rise
☐ 桜 cherry
☐ うずうずする itch
☐ 梅 plum
☐ 桃 peach
☐ 禅宗 Zen Buddhist
☐ 鯛 sea bream
☐ 小袖 short sleeved kimono
☐ もみじ maple leaf

Ohanami was also encouraged by those in power

The most magnificent *ohanami* party in Japanese history is said to be the "Blossom Viewing at Daigo" held by Chancellor Toyotomi Hideyoshi in 1598 at Daigoji temple in Kyoto. Around three thousand people, from court nobles and samurais to commoners, came to enjoy the attractions, including a banquet and fancy dress parade. The Edo-period shogun Tokugawa Yoshimune (1684–1751) planted cherry trees at various places in Edo, including the banks of the Sumida River, Asukayama (Ōji), and Gotenyama (Shinagawa), creating recreational spaces for the citizens.

☐ 盛大な magnificent
☐ 関白 Chancellor
☐ 公家 court noble
☐ 庶民 commoner
☐ 宴会 banquet
☐ 仮装行列 fancy dress parade
☐ 堤 bank
☐ 憩いの場 recreational space

「場所取り」は新人の役目？

お花見は職場仲間や大学のサークル仲間などでも催されるが、眺めが良くて宴会に向いた場所を確保する「場所取り」は、たいてい新しく入った社員や学生の役目である。一種の入会儀式（イニシエーション）にもなっている。適当な新人を確保できないチームのために、「場所取り代行ビジネス」も登場している。（皇居近くの北の丸公園では、約100人規模の場所取りサービスで10万円近くかかることも！）

こうなると、どうも桜は口実であって、日本人は宴会好きだということかもしれない。米国のワシントンDCにあるポトマック河畔の桜並木は、1912年に日本から贈られた苗木が育ったもので、やはり多くの人が「お花見」に集まるというが、宴会にはならない。

Reserving a space is the role of junior members

Work colleagues and university club members also hold *ohanami* parties, and in order to ensure a good spot for the party the newest employee or member is sent to reserve a space. This is a kind of initiation rite. There are also businesses that specialize in fulfilling this role when there is no appropriate rookie to send. At Kitanomaru Park near the Imperial Palace, a space-reserving service for around 100 people can cost nearly 100,000 yen!

When it comes down to it, blossom viewing is probably just an excuse for Japanese people to hold a party. The cherry blossoms on the banks of the Potomac River in Washington D.C. were gifted as saplings by Japan in 1912, and while of course many people go to admire them, they don't hold parties under the trees.

□職場仲間 work colleague

□大学のサークル仲間 university club member

□催す hold

□(場所)を確保する ensure

□場所取り reserve a place

□入会儀式 initiation rite

□適当な appropriate

□(人)を確保する secure

□皇居 Imperial Palace

□こうなると when it comes down to it

□口実 excuse

□河畔 riverbank

□苗木 sapling

4. 節句

1年間に5日、固有の行事がある節句

　古代中国の**陰陽思想**には数字への**信仰**がある。**偶数**は**安定**して**静的**であるので陰の数字、**奇数**は**不安定**で**動的**であることから陽の数字とされ、奇数(陽)の方が縁起が良いとされた。しかし陽と陽が重なると陰に転じ**厄災**を生じやすくなる。それが1年間の奇数月の**特定**の奇数日を重視することになり、**厄を払う行事を行う**ようになった。季節の節目でもあることから「**節句**」(節供あるいは節会とも)と呼ばれるようになった。陽の数字の最大は9なので11月を除くと1年に5日の「**節句**」があることになり、日本では江戸幕府が五節句の祝日とし、それぞれの**行事**が**根付く**ことになった。

1月7日は「人日の節句」

　古代中国では1月のはじめの7日間に、鶏、犬、豚、羊、牛、馬、人を**割り当て**、その天候からその年のそれぞれの**吉凶**を占った。またその日はその動物を食べてはならない日とされ、人の日(人日)つまり1月7日は罪人の処罰をしない日とされた。またこの日は7種類の**野草**を入れた**羹**(テリーヌ)を食べる習慣もあった。これが日本に伝わってからは、「七草がゆ」を食べる日となった。

4. Seasonal Festivals

Five particular festivals during the year

Numbers were important in the yin-yang ideology of ancient China, with even numbers considered stable and static, and therefore yin, while odd numbers are unstable and dynamic and therefore yang. Odd numbers (yang) were considered luckier, but yang plus yang become yin and more prone to bring about misfortune. This is why specific odd-numbered days in odd-numbered months are emphasized and events held to ward off misfortune. Since these also coincide with changes in the season, they are also called *sekku* (or sometimes *sechie*), "seasonal festivals." The largest yang number is 9, so if we discount November (the eleventh month) and only count the other odd-numbered months, there are five of these seasonal festivals during the year. The Edo-period shogunate celebrated these *gosekku* (five seasonal festivals) with specific events for each that have become ingrained in Japanese culture.

□ 陰陽思想 yin-yang ideology
□ 偶数 even number
□ 安定した stable
□ 静的な static
□ 奇数 odd number
□ 不安定な unstable
□ 動的な dynamic
□ 厄災 misfortune
□ 生じやすい prone to bring about
□ 特定の specific
□ 厄を払う ward off misfortune
□ 根付く become ingrained

January 7: *Jinjitsu*, or "Day of Mankind"

In ancient China, the first seven days of the first month were designated rooster, dog, boar, sheep, ox, horse, and human, and the fortune of the year was divined according to the weather on those days. Further, it was decreed that on these days the animal concerned should not be harmed, and on the seventh day (for humans), criminals would go unpunished. There was also the custom of eating a hot soup containing seven different herbs, a practice which reached Japan, where it has become the day to eat *nanakusa-gayu* (rice gruel with seven herbs).

□ 割り当てる designate
□ 吉凶 fortune
□ 占う divine
□ 罪人 criminal
□ 処罰をしない unpunished
□ 野草 herb
□ 羹 broth made of fish and vegetables
□ かゆ rice gruel

3月3日は「上巳の節句」

中国では3月上旬の巳の日、川のほとりで厄を払う儀式を行ったり、水に浮かべた盃が自分のところに着くまでに歌を詠む「曲水の宴」を行った。日本の宮中にも取り入れられた。そのうち厄払いの部分を紙で作った人形で行うようになり、女の子の「ひな祭り」にと変形して庶民の間にも広がった。この季節に咲く花から「桃の節句」ともいう。

人の姿をかたどった「ひな人形」に穢れを移し、難を逃れる厄除けにする

Impurity (*kegare*) is transferred to dolls called *hina ningyō* to ward off misfortune.

5月5日は「端午の節句」

5月の始め(端)の午の日は、中国では「ちまき」を食べる。紀元前3世紀の楚の重臣だった屈原が失脚して悲嘆のあまり入水自殺した日だが、屈原を慕う人々が遺体が魚に食べられぬようにちまきを投げ込んで供養したとの伝説がある。また菖蒲やよもぎの葉で邪気を払う風習もあったという。日本では鎌倉時代に「菖蒲(武を貴ぶ尚武と同じ読み)の節句」つまり男の子の節句とされるようになり武者人形を飾るようになったという。またのちには、滝をのぼる鯉が龍になるという中国の出世伝説も取り入れて、鯉幟を立てる風習も加わった。

鯉幟
carp streamer

March 3: *Jōshi*, or "First Day of the Snake"

In China, on the first Day of the Snake in the third month, a ceremony would be conducted on the banks of a stream to drive away ill fortune, and parties known as "winding stream banquets" would be held in which participants had to compose a poem before a wine cup floating on the current reached them. This was also introduced into the Imperial Court in Japan. It was around this time that a human figure cut out of paper began to be used in the ceremony to banish ill fortune, and this developed into the *hina matsuri* "Dolls Festival" for girls that is widely celebrated today. It is also known as the Peach Festival, named after the blossoms that bloom at this time.

□巳の日 Day of the Snake

□川ほとり bank of a stream

□厄を払う drive away ill fortune

□儀式 ceremony

□盃 wine cup

□歌を詠む compose a poem

□曲水の宴 winding stream banquet

□宮中 Imperial Court

□厄払い ceremony to banish ill fortune

□人形（ひとがた） human figure

May 5: *Tango*, or "First Day of the Horse"

In China, *chimaki* rice dumplings wrapped in bamboo leaves are eaten on the first Day of the Horse of the fifth month. According to legend this is the day on which, in the third century BC, the senior Chu statesman Qu Yuan became so anguished after his fall from power that he drowned himself, and his followers threw *chimaki* dumplings into the water to distract the fish from eating his body, and held a memorial service for him. There was also a custom whereby misfortune was driven out with irises and mugwort leaves. In the Kamakura period, it was known as *shōbu no hi* or "day of the iris" (*shōbu* is a homophone for "iris" and "military prowess") and was a day for boys, celebrated with displays of warrior dolls. Later still, the Chinese legend of a carp that succeeded in climbing a waterfall to become a dragon developed into the custom of hanging out carp streamers.

□午の日 Day of the Horse

□ちまき rice dumplings wrapped in bamboo leaves

□紀元前 BC

□失脚する fall from power

□悲嘆のあまり become so anguished

□入水自殺する drown oneself

□遺体 body

□供養する hold memorial service

□伝説 legend

□菖蒲 iris

□よもぎ mugwort

□邪気 misfortune

□武者人形 warrior doll

□滝 waterfall

□鯉幟 carp streamer

7月7日は「七夕の節句」

天の河を挟んで片方には**牛飼い**の牽牛という男がおり、他方に天女の衣を織る**織女**がいた。働きづめの二人を**憐れんだ**天帝が**結婚**を許したが幸せのあまり織女は**機織り**を忘れた。怒った天帝は二人を引き離し、1年に1度しか会えなくした。これが中国の「棚機伝説」であり、**裁縫の上達**を祈る乞巧奠行事やお盆行事とも結びついた。日本に入ってからは**技芸の上達**や良縁を願った短冊を笹の葉に結んで飾る「七夕」の行事になった。

短冊に願いごとを書いて
星にお祈りする

People write their wishes
on strips of paper and pray
to the stars.

9月9日は「重陽の節句」

9は最大の陽の数字。それが**重なる**と陰に転じ大きな**災厄を招き**かねない。その厄を払って**長寿**を祈るために、季節の花である菊を酒に浮かべて飲んだり、菊の露をしみこませた**綿**で体をぬぐうといった習慣が行われていた。また、茱萸の袋を腕に結び、菊の香の酒を持って**郊外の小高い丘**(天に近い!)にピクニックに出かける習慣(登高)もあった。

July 7: *Tanabata*, or the "Star Festival"

In the heavens two lovers, a cowherd and a weaver maid, dwell either side of the Milky Way. The Lord of Heaven had taken pity on the hardworking couple and allowed them to marry, but they were so happy that the weaver maid forgot about her weaving. In a rage, the Lord of Heaven separated them and thenceforth allowed them to meet only once a year. This Chinese legend is linked also to the *kikkōden* festival to pray for dexterity in needlework and to *Obon* traditions. Since arriving in Japan, it has become an event where people write wishes for handicraft skills and favorable matches on strips of paper that they hang on bamboo grass.

- □ 天の河 Milky Way
- □ 牛飼い cowherd
- □ 天女の衣 heavenly garment
- □ 織女 weaver maid
- □ 憐れむ take pity
- □ 天帝 the Lord of Heaven
- □ 結婚 marry
- □ 機織り weaving
- □ 裁縫 needlework
- □ 技芸 handicraft skill
- □ 良縁 favorable match
- □ 笹の葉 bamboo grass

September 9: *Chōyō*, or the "Chrysanthemum Festival"

Nine is the highest yang number. When doubled, it changes to yin and is capable of attracting great misfortune. Customs to dispel this misfortune and pray for longevity included drinking sake on which the season's flower, the chrysanthemum, had been floated, and wiping one's body with cotton steeped in dew from chrysanthemums. There was also a custom (called *tōkō*, or "climbing to a height") of dangling a bag of Japanese pepper from one's arm, taking chrysanthemum-scented sake, and going to a small hill outside town for a picnic.

- □ 重なる double
- □ 転じる change
- □ 災厄 misfortune
- □ 〜を招きかねない capable of attracting
- □ 長寿 longevity
- □ 菊 chrysanthemum
- □ 露 dew
- □ しみこませる steep in
- □ 綿 cotton
- □ ぬぐう wipe
- □ 郊外 outside town
- □ 小高い丘 small hill

5. お彼岸

05

年に2度、先祖の墓参りをする日

　昼と夜の長さが同じになる日が年間に2度ある。春の春分の日（3月21日頃）と秋の秋分の日（9月23日頃）で、国民の**移動祝日**になっている。これらの日を挟んだ前後3日、計7日間が「お彼岸」で、**先祖の墓参りをする**習慣がある。これはほかの**仏教圏**にはない。

　また、このお彼岸辺りから気温が大きく変化することから、「暑さ寒さも彼岸まで」ということわざもある。

　お彼岸という言葉は仏教用語の「**彼岸・此岸**」から来たもので、**煩悩**を脱した**極楽**の世界が彼岸、**苦しみと迷い**に満ちた現世が此岸。死者である先祖は彼岸に暮らしている。

必須のお供え物アイテムは？

　お彼岸に用意する**お供えもの**としては、蒸し米を半分ついた餅にあずきなどの**餡**をからめたもの。春の彼岸には「**牡丹餅**」と呼ばれ、秋の彼岸には「**おはぎ**」と呼ばれる。**甘味**の乏しい暮らしをしていた昔の日本人にとって、年に2度しか食べられなかったこの「**牡丹餅**」は大変なごちそうだった。そこから、苦労せずに**おもいがけない**幸運が舞い込むという意味の、「棚からぼたもち」ということわざも生まれた。

5. *Ohigan*: Equinoctial Weeks

Two annual visits to the graves of ancestors

There are two days every year when day and night are the same length. The Spring Equinox (around March 21) and Autumn Equinox (around September 23) are movable national holidays in Japan. The three days before and after the equinoctial days, seven days in all, are called *ohigan*, when it is customary for people to visit the graves of their ancestors. This custom is not practiced in other Buddhist countries.

Also, due to the major changes in temperature around the time of *ohigan*, there is a saying, "Neither heat nor cold lasts beyond the equinox."

The word *ohigan* comes from the Buddhist term for "the other world" (or afterlife, as opposed to *shigan*, "this world"), where the other world is a paradise in which we are freed of earthly desires, while this life is full of suffering and delusion. Our ancestors, having passed away, live in the other world.

☐ 移動祝日 movable national holiday
☐ 先祖 ancestor
☐ 墓参り visit the grave
☐ 気温 temperature
☐ 彼岸 the other world, afterlife
☐ 此岸 this world
☐ 煩悩 earthly desire
☐ 極楽 paradise
☐ 苦しみ suffering
☐ 迷い delusion

Essential items for the offering

Rice cakes mixed with steamed rice and rolled in red bean paste are prepared as offerings at *ohigan*. In spring these are called *bota mochi*, and in autumn *ohagi*. In the past, Japanese had very few sweets, and these rice cakes that were eaten only twice a year were a real treat. This gave rise to the saying *Tana kara bota mochi* ("A *bota-mochi* falls from the shelf") to refer to a stroke of unexpected good fortune or a windfall.

☐ お供えもの offering
☐ 蒸し米 steamed rice
☐ あずき red bean
☐ 餡 bean paste
☐ 甘味 sweets
☐ ごちそう treat
☐ おもいがけない unexpected
☐ ことわざ saying

春のお彼岸では「牡丹餅」、秋のお彼岸では「お萩」と言う

At the spring equinox these are called *bota mochi*, and at the autumn equinox *ohagi*.

6. 夏の土用

06

夏のスタミナ補給には「ウナギ」

　陰陽五行の説によれば、世界は「木・火・土・金・水」の5つの成分で構成され、それぞれが季節によって交代しながら気を支配するという。春は木、夏は火、秋は金、冬は水であるが、その季節の変わり目ごとに支配的になるのが土である。しかし、そんな細切れに配される土の気のことは忘れられて、立秋前の夏の土用(約18日間)だけが日本人の関心を集めるようになった。蒸し暑く、誰もが元気をなくす季節なのだが、特別な食べ物がそのスタミナを補給してくれると信じられているからだ。この食べ物は、とくに土用18日間のうちの「丑の日」に食べるのがよいとされる。そう、甘辛いタレで焼いたウナギである。

　「ウナギを食べて夏を乗り切ろう」という宣伝文句を考え出した人物もわかっている。植物学者で戯作者で発明家で画家でもあったマルチタレントの平賀源内(1728-1779)だ。ただ、稚魚の不漁が続く昨今ではウナギも庶民の手が届かない高級品になっている。

6. *Doyō*: The Hottest Part of Summer

Eel boosts stamina in summer

According to the doctrine of yin yang and the five elements, the earth is made up of the five elements wood, fire, earth, metal, and water which change according to the season and influence our mood. Spring is wood, summer is fire, autumn is metal, and winter is water, while the dominant element at each turn of season is earth. However, this periodic dominance of earth has been largely forgotten, and now Japanese people are only concerned with its effect in the *doyō* season, the hottest part of summer before the start of fall (about eighteen days). This is because they believe in the power of a certain food to boost stamina in this hot, humid season when everyone lacks energy. It is particularly thought to be good to eat on the Day of the Ox that falls within the eighteen-day *doyō* period. That's right: fried eel served in a salt-sweet sauce!

It is also known that the catchphrase "Let's eat eel to get through summer!" was coined by the multitalented Hiraga Gennai (1728–1780), a botanist, popular novelist, inventor, and painter. However, these days when even catches of fish fry are persistently poor, eel is also becoming a delicacy beyond the reach of ordinary people.

☐ 説 doctrine
☐ 木 wood
☐ 火 fire
☐ 土 earth
☐ 金 metal
☐ 水 water
☐ 季節 season
☐ 立秋 start of fall
☐ 蒸し暑い hot and humid
☐ (スタミナを)補給する boost
☐ 丑の日 Day of the Ox
☐ 甘辛い salt-sweet
☐ ウナギ eel
☐ 乗り切る get through
☐ 宣伝文句 catchphrase
☐ 植物学者 botanist
☐ 戯作者 novelist
☐ 発明家 inventor
☐ 画家 painter
☐ 稚魚 fish fry
☐ 昨今 these days

うな重 *Unaju,* grilled eel on rice

7. お盆

07

死者の霊を供養する夏の行事

　地方によって異なるが、7月または8月の13日から16日の間に、亡くなった祖先、家族の霊を迎え、供養し、送り返す一連の行事のこと。とくに亡くなって1年未満の死者の場合は「新盆」と称して、僧侶に読経してもらうなど手厚く供養する。霊を迎えたり、送る際には夕方に玄関などで火を炊くのが一般的だが、位牌や墓前への供養の仕方や飾りは仏教宗派によって異なる。浄土宗などではきゅうりやナスとキビがらで作った馬や牛を供えたり、ほおずきを吊るしたり、蓮の葉に食べ物を置いたりする。

　お盆は仏教界では「盂蘭盆会」という。「会」は仏教行事の意味だが、「うらぼん」はサンスクリット語で「逆さづり（の苦しみ）」だとの説もあるがはっきりしない。

お盆の飾り
Decoration the Buddhist alter in Obon

国民的夏休みと盆踊り

　新暦の8月15日前後は、夏の休暇を取る人、実家のある故郷に帰省する人が多いために、実質的に国民的な夏休みになっている。また、お盆の中日である15日あたりには、集落の空き地や寺社の境内、学校のグラウンドなどに櫓を組んで、それを囲むようにして回りながら踊る盆踊りが各地で催される。歌われるのがその地域に伝わる民謡だったりすることが多く、帰省した人々などはノスタルジックな気分を楽しめる。

7. Obon

Summer events to honor the spirits of the dead

Obon customs vary according to region, but are generally a series of events held from the 13th to the 16th of either July or August to welcome back the spirits of family members who have passed away, make offerings to them, and send them back again. Particular consideration is shown by getting a priest to chant sutras for them, especially for those who died within the past year, called *niibon*. Fires are commonly lit at the entrance to houses in the evening to welcome the spirits and to see them off again, but the ways of making offerings and decorating the memorial tablets and graves vary according to the Buddhist sect. In Pure Land and some other sects, offerings of horse or cow figurines made from cucumber or eggplant and millet, hanging Japanese lantern plants, and food placed on lotus leaves.

In Buddhist circles *Obon* is called *Urabon-e*, the *Bon Festival*. The *e* refers to a Buddhist festival, while there is a theory that *urabon* comes from a Sanskrit word meaning "(the pain of) hanging upside down," although this is not clear.

A national summer holiday and the *bon-odori* dance

Around August 15, many people take holidays and travel back to their hometown to visit the family home, effectively making it a national summer vacation. Also, on the 15th, at the height of *Obon*, a scaffold platform is set up on a vacant lot in the community, in the precincts of shrines or temples, or on school grounds, and the local people dance the *bon-odori* in a circle around it. People often sing local folk songs, and those returning from far away enjoy feeling nostalgic.

- □ 地方 region
- □ 祖先 ancestor
- □ 供養する make an offering
- □ 一連の a series of
- □ 読経する chant a sutra
- □ 手厚さ particular consideration
- □ 位牌 memorial tablet
- □ きゅうり cucumber
- □ ナス eggplant
- □ キビ millet
- □ ほおずき Japanese lantern plant
- □ 蓮 lotus
- □ 逆さづり hanging upside down

- □ 実家 family home
- □ 故郷 hometown
- □ 空き地 vacant lot
- □ 櫓 scaffold platform
- □ 民謡 folk song

ぼんおど
盆踊り

People dance the *bon-odori*.

8. お月見

08

「十五夜」と「十三夜」の違い

　旧暦の秋は7〜9月。そのど真ん中である8月15日に出るのが中秋の月（十五夜）。この月を観賞する行事が「お月見」であるが、「お花見」と違って酒宴とは結びつかない。ルーツは中国で、本来月を愛でる風流な行事（中秋節）だったものが、現代になって祝日になり、お菓子の「月餅」の大ギフト月間にヒートアップしている。日本では、ススキの穂や月見団子、サトイモ、枝豆などを飾る程度。収穫祭でもあったから別名「芋名月」。

　翌月の9月13日にもやはり月への供え物をし、月を愛でる。これが「十三夜」。供え物の主役が栗になったりするので別名「栗名月」。かつては、この「十五夜」と「十三夜」の両方を見ないで片方だけ見るのを、「片見月」と呼んで嫌った。

お月見のイメージ：満月に見立てた丸い団子を飾る

At otsukimi, a round dumplings is generally decorated to resemble a full moon.

8. *Otsukimi*: Moon Viewing

The difference between the Fifteenth Night and the Thirteenth Night

Under the old lunar calendar, autumn covered the period from the seventh to the ninth months. The mid-autumn moon comes right in the middle of this period, on the fifteenth of the eighth month, (the Fifteenth Night). This falls in September under the solar calendar, and moon-viewing events are called *otsukimi*, but unlike *ohanami* blossom viewing, do not involve drinking and feasting. It has its roots in China, and originally was a refined occasion to admire the full moon during the mid-autumn festival, but these days it is a public holiday and people give gifts of sweet round cakes called *geppei* during the month leading up to it. In Japan, there are displays of pampas grass, *tsukimi-dango* "full-moon dumplings," taro potatoes, and *edamame*. This was also a harvest festival, so another name for it is *imomeigetsu*, literally "beautiful potato-moon."

On the thirteenth of the ninth month (October in the solar calendar) offerings are again made in admiration of the full moon. This is the Thirteenth Night. The most popular offerings are chestnuts, so it is also known as the *kurimeigetsu*, or "beautiful chestnut moon." In the past, viewing only one or the other full moons of the Fifteenth and Thirteenth Nights was known as *katamitsuki*, or single moon viewing, and was frowned upon.

.

□旧暦 old lunar calendar

□中秋の月 mid-autumn moon

□月を鑑賞する moon-viewing

□行事 event, occasion

□本来 originally

□愛でる admire

□風流な refined

□月餅 mooncake

□ススキ pampas grass

□団子 dumplings

□サトイモ taro potato

□程度 only, enough

□収穫祭 harvest festival

□栗 chestnut

月見とハンバーガー

　満月の色と形から、「黄色くて円いもの」を「月見〜」と名付けることが多い。食品では**卵の黄身**がそうで、卵を落としたうどんは「月見うどん」、**目玉焼き**を乗せたハンバーガーは「月見ハンバーガー」になる。こういう**発想**は、月光を浴びると**狂気**を発するとか**狼男**に変身するといった伝説を持つ**欧米**とはだいぶ違う。

月に住むのはウサギかカエルか

　日本の**童謡**に「ウサギ、ウサギ、何見て**跳**ねる。十五夜お月さん見て跳ねる」というのがある。月とウサギは**縁**が深いと考えられており、月のクレーターが作り出す**陰影**を見て「ウサギが**杵**を持って**臼**で**餅**つきしている**様子**」にたとえてきた（ちょっと無理があるが）。中国では餅でなく**仙薬**をついているウサギというし、別の伝説では**不老不死の薬**を盗んで月に逃げたために**ヒキガエル**にされた**悪妻**、嫦娥だともいわれる。

　月にウサギの姿を刻んだのは帝釈天だというインドの**仏教説話**がある。**内容**は、**行き倒れ**の老人を救うために、ウサギが「自分を食べて」と火中に飛び込んだ。それに**感銘**をうけた老人、実は帝釈天が、その**献身**を**讃え**てウサギを月に**送った**という。これは「今昔物語集」という日本の説話集にも**採録**された。また、日本最古の物語「竹取物語」は、月から使わされた「かぐや姫」が、**成人**して月に帰って行くまでの話である。月を見る日本人の感性はあくまでもロマンチックかつ**感傷的な**ようだ。

Moon-viewing hamburgers

Many things that are yellow and round are labeled "moon view-ing" after the shape and color of the full moon. This includes egg yolks, so noodles with an egg yolk on top are known as "moon-viewing noodles," and a fried egg on a hamburger makes a "moon-viewing hamburger." This concept is quite different from the Western association of moonlight with madness (lunatics) and the legend of transforming into a werewolf.

□卵の黄身 egg yolk
□目玉焼き fried egg
□発想 concept
□月光 moonlight
□狂気 madness, lunatics
□狼男 werewolf

Is it a rabbit or a toad living on the moon?

A Japanese nursery rhyme goes "Rabbit, O Rabbit, what makes you jump for joy? See? The big round moon makes me jump for joy." There is thought to be a strong connection between rabbits and the moon, and the shadows created by the moon's craters have been likened to a rabbit pounding rice with a mallet and mortar (somewhat implausibly). In China the rabbit is making not *mochi* but an elixir, and in a different legend, it is the bad wife Chang'e, who was transformed into a toad after stealing an elixir of life and fleeing to the moon.

According to a Buddhist tale from India, Taishakuten carved the image of a rabbit onto the moon. The rabbit had saved an old man who had fainted by telling him "Eat me!" before jumping into a fire. The old man had in fact been Taishakuten, lord of Heaven, who was so impressed that he praised the rabbit for its self-sacrifice and sent it to the moon. This tale is also recorded in the *Konjaku monogatarishū*, "Anthology of Tales from the Past." Japan's earliest known tale, *Taketori monogatari* ("Tale of the Bamboo Cutter") is about Princess Kaguya who was from the moon and returned there upon becoming an adult. Japanese people seem to become very romantic, and even sentimental, when they gaze at the moon!

□童謡 nursery rhyme
□跳ねる jump
□縁 connection
□陰影 shadow
□杵 mallet
□臼 mortar
□餅つきする pound rice
□たとえる liken
□仙薬 elixir
□不老不死の薬 elixir of life
□ヒキガエル toad
□行き倒れする faint
□感銘をうける be impressed
□献身 self-sacrifice
□讃える praise
□採録される be recorded
□成人 adult
□感傷的な sentimental

9. お祭り

09

豊作を祈る春、豊作を感謝する秋

　税や給与が米や魚などの農林水産物で支払われていた江戸時代までの日本では、毎年の作物のでき具合や漁の水揚げ高が死活問題だった。虫の害や気候変動にも無力だった。そのため農作業や漁を始める春先には神仏に祈り、供物を出して祀るしかなかった。そして期待通りの豊作や豊漁があれば、その神仏に感謝を捧げた。集落単位のこの行事が春や秋の祭りであり、その起源は世界中で似たようなものだったはずだ。

　幸運な年が続けばゆとりが生まれ、祭りにも彩りが加わる。そろいの浴衣や法被を身に付け、神輿をかつぎ、鉦や太鼓や笛のお囃子が付き、引き回される山車には歌い手や踊り手が乗せられた。提灯がゆらめき、屋台店が並び、人々が踊りの輪に加わり、水辺から花火が打ち上げられて夜空に大輪の火の華をひらいた……。

　その土地固有の物語や歴史や美意識が加味されて、全国各地に個性豊かな祭りが生まれた。しかし21世紀に入った日本では、祭りとその担い手が急速に失われつつある。

9. *Omatsuri*: Festivals

In spring to pray for a good harvest, in fall to give thanks for the harvest

Until the Edo period taxes and salaries were paid in agricultural and marine produce, such as rice and fish, so crop yields and fish catches were a matter of life or death. People were powerless against insect damage and weather variability, and so all they could do was to pray and make offerings to the gods and Buddha in early spring before the start of the farming and fishing seasons. And then, if they achieved bumper crops and catches as hoped for, they would offer thanks to the gods and Buddha. These events held in villages are the spring and summer festivals, and their origins must have been similar the world over.

When several good years follow in succession, people become better off and the festivals become more elaborate. They dress in matching *yukata* and *happi* coats, carry the *mikoshi* shrine, play festival music with gongs, drums, and flutes, and festival floats carry singers and dancers. Paper lanterns are lit, stalls are set up, people join in the circle of dancers, and the night sky is lit up by fireworks set off from the waters edge…

Local tales, history, and aesthetic sense add flavor to the occasion, making these festivals unique around the country. In the twenty-first century, however, the festivals and their supporters are rapidly disappearing.

- □ 税 tax
- □ 給与 salary
- □ 農林水産物 agricultural and marine produce
- □ 作物のでき具合 crop yield
- □ 漁の水揚げ高 fish catch
- □ 死活問題 matter of life or death
- □ 虫の害 insect damage
- □ 気候変動 weather variability
- □ 神仏 gods and Buddha
- □ 供物 offering
- □ 祀る worship
- □ 鉦 gong
- □ お囃子 festival music
- □ 山車 festival float
- □ 提灯 paper lantern
- □ 屋台店 stall
- □ 花火 firework
- □ 美意識 aesthetic sense
- □ 全国各地に around the country
- □ 担い手 supporter

10. 大晦日
<ruby>大晦日<rt>おお みそ か</rt></ruby>

10

1年の最後の夜の過ごし方
<ruby>1年<rt>ねん</rt></ruby>の<ruby>最後<rt>さいご</rt></ruby>の<ruby>夜<rt>よる</rt></ruby>の<ruby>過<rt>す</rt></ruby>ごし<ruby>方<rt>かた</rt></ruby>

　「おおみそか」の「みそか(晦日)」というのは「三十日」つまり月末のことであり、12月の月末は1年の最後の日なので「大みそか」または「大つごもり」という。「つごもり」は「月が出なくなる」＝「月隠り」からきている。

　1年最後の日は大掃除の締めくくりとなる「掃き納め」や、おせち料理を作って、お正月の準備を整える。

　そして夜食に出されるのが「そば」である。そばの実は世界各地で使われている食材だが、粉を練ってから切って麺状にする「そば切り」は、日本では16世紀頃に生まれた食べ方とされる。「細く長く生きられますように」という江戸風のダジャレだ。その江戸時代には元旦に食べたともいわれる。

10. *Ōmisoka*: New Year's Eve

The very last night of the year

Misoka, literally "thirtieth day," refers to the end of the month, and this is prefixed with *ō*, meaning "great," to indicate the last day of the twelfth month—that is, the very last day of the year. Another word for this is *ō-tsugomori, tsugomori* meaning literally "hidden moon" and also refers to the last day of the month—or of the year, when prefixed with *ō*.

On the last day of the year, a big cleanup is concluded with a "final sweeping," after which people begin to make *osechi ryōri* and prepare for the new year.

Dinner is *soba* noodles. *Soba*, or buckwheat, is grown all over the world, but it is thought that the method of kneading the flour into dough then cutting it into noodles started in the sixteenth century. In a corny Edo-style pun, the long, thin noodles are said to represent the desire to live a long and frugal life. They were apparently eaten on New Year's Day during the Edo period.

□月末 the end of the month

□隠り hiding

□締めくくりとなる be concluded

□納め the last

□そばの実 buckwheat's seed

□粉 flour

□練る knead

□切って麺状にする cut something into noodles

□江戸風の Edo-style

□ダジャレ pun

除夜の鐘と「2年参り」

　大みそかの夜は別名「除夜」ともいう。1年の間に重なった厄災を除くという意味だ。大きな寺では鐘楼の鐘を108回打ち鳴らす。108というのは人間が持つ**食欲・金銭欲・色欲**などの**煩悩**の数とされる。この108回を年内につき終えるか、**年をまたぐ**か、新年になってからつくかは寺によって異なる。また、普通は年が明けてから行う「**初詣で**」を、大みそかの夜から来てお参りするのを「**2年参り**」という。

寺の鐘

A temple bell

Ringing out the old year, and *ni-nen mairi*

Another word for New Year's Eve is *joya*, which means removing all the misfortunes of the year. In major temples, the temple bell is rung 108 times. This represents the number of earthly desires, such as greed, avarice, and lust, that people have. Whether ringing the bell is completed within the old year, straddles the year, or wholly in the New Year varies according to the temple. Also, when the *hatsumōde*, or first shrine visit of the New Year, is started on New Year's Eve and continues into the New Year, it is called *ni-nen mairi*, or "two-year visit" (to see out the old year, and welcome the new year).

☐ 鐘楼 belfry

☐ 食欲 greed

☐ 金銭欲 avarice

☐ 色欲 lust

☐ 煩悩 earthly desires

☐ 年をまたぐ straddle the year

☐ 初詣で first shrine visit of the year

2
じんせい
人生
Life Events

1. 出産
しゅっさん

11

妊娠5ヵ月目に妊婦がすること
にんしん　　げつめ　にんぷ

　東京の日本橋蛎殻町に水天宮という神社がある。九州の久留米市に本宮があって子供と水の守り神とされるが、月に2、3度ある「戌の日」となると、若い女性とその親や夫らしき人との参拝客で大変な賑わいになる。参拝客の目的は同じで、「子供を授かりたい」「安産でありたい」あるいは「無事に出産できたことを感謝したい」というもの。「戌の日」がとくに混雑するのは、犬が安産・多産だと信じられているからだ。女性たちはここに来て安産の祈禱をしてもらったり、「岩田帯」を買い求めたりする。

　「岩田帯」というのは木綿の長い帯であり、「岩田」は「結肌」「斎肌」がなまったものと言われる。妊婦と胎児に取り付きやすい災厄や事故から守るため、妊娠5ヵ月目に入った女性が腹部を保護するために巻くのである。

水天宮の「子宝いぬ」
Kodakara dog at Suitengū shrine

1. Birth

What women do in the fifth month of pregnancy

In the Kakigarachō district of Nihonbashi in Tokyo, there is a shrine called Suitengū. It is a branch of the main temple in Kurume, Kyushu, and is dedicated to protecting children and to water, but two or three times a month on the Day of the Dog, it is crowded with young women visiting the shrine accompanied by their parents and husbands. They all have the same objectives: "Please let me be blessed with children," "Please give me an easy delivery," or "Thank you for letting me give birth safely." The reason the shrine is particularly busy on the Day of the Dog is that the dog is believed to give birth many times without problems. Women come here to have prayers said for safe delivery and to purchase *iwata-obi* maternity bands.

The *iwata-obi* is a long cotton band, and its name, written with the kanji for "rock" and "field," is thought to be a dialect corruption of another word referring to supporting or purifying the skin. Women wear it around their belly from the fifth month of pregnancy to protect themselves and their baby from misfortune and accidents.

- □ 本宮 main temple
- □ 戌の日 the Day of the Dog
- □ 参拝客 visitor
- □ 目的 objective
- □ 子供を授かる be blessed with children
- □ 安産 easy delivery
- □ 出産する give birth
- □ 祈禱 prayer
- □ 木綿 cotton
- □ 帯 band
- □ 妊婦 pregnant woman
- □ 胎児 fetus
- □ 災厄 misfortune
- □ 妊娠 pregnancy

生後100日目の乳児に石を食べさせる？

　かつて妊娠・出産は穢れ多きものと見なされた。でも本当は、そうして特別に慎重に対処することで母体と新生児が清潔・健康に過ごせるようにと願ったからだといわれる。それは誕生後の様々な行事があることからもうかがえる。たとえば生まれて7日目の夜は「お七夜」といい、赤ちゃんに命名する儀式がある。法律的には出産後14日以内に役所に届ければ良いのだが、両親を含めてこの儀式を行う夫婦は少なくない。また、ほぼひと月たつと、子供の誕生を近所の氏神様に報告する「お宮参り」がある。そして100日目には「お食い初め」の儀式があり、ご馳走を用意し、子供が一生、食べるもので困らないようにと願う。ユニークなのは、食膳に小さな石が添えてあることで、やがて生えそろう歯が石のように丈夫でありますようにというまじないである。

Are 100-day-old babies fed stones?

In the past, pregnancy and childbirth were considered unclean. The truth is, though, that this meant they were handled sensitively and special attention paid to the health and cleanliness of the mother and her newborn baby. This is also evident in the various events held following the birth. For example, the seventh night after birth is called *oshichiya*, and is when a naming ceremony is held for the baby. Legally, the birth should be registered within fourteen days, but more than a few couples hold this ceremony together with their parents. Also, about a month after birth, a shrine visit is made to inform the local deity of the child's birth. And on the 100th day, a weaning ceremony is held, for which a feast is prepared and prayers given that the child will never lack for food. A unique feature of this is a small stone or stones placed on the dining table as a talisman for the baby to grow strong, healthy teeth.

□出産 childbirth
□穢れ多き unclean
□対処する handle
□新生児 newborn baby
□命名する儀式 naming ceremony
□法律的には legally
□氏神様 deity
□お宮参り shrine visit
□「お食い初め」の儀式 weaning ceremony
□ご馳走 feast
□食膳 dining table
□添える garnish
□まじない talisman

2. 七五三
しち ご さん

12

7歳まで無事に育てばひと安心
なな さい　　　ぶ じ　そだ　　　　　　　あんしん

　こうして**乳児期を無事に乗り切って**も、まだまだ安心はできないのが親
にゅうじ き　　ぶ じ　の　き　　　　　　　　　　　　あんしん　　　　　　　　　　　　　おや
心。何しろ「7つ前は神のうち」という言葉があるくらい、**乳幼児の成育**は
ごころ　なに　　　　　　なな まえ　かみ　　　　　　　　　　こと ば　　　　　　　　　　　にゅうようじ　せいいく
神様しだいと思われていた。そこで日本では3歳、5歳、7歳と**奇数年齢**を
かみさま　　　　　　おも　　　　　　　　　　　　　に ほん　　　さい　　さい　　さい　　き すうねんれい
目安にして、神仏に無事な成長を祈る「七五三」の儀式が**普及**した。地方
め やす　　　　　　しんぶつ　ぶ じ　せいちょう　いの　　しち ご さん　　ぎ しき　　ふ きゅう　　　　　ち ほう
によって違いはあるものの、女の子は3歳と7歳、男の子は3歳と5歳になっ
　　　　　ちが　　　　　　　　　　おんな　こ　　さい　　さい おとこ　こ　　さい　　さい
た年の11月15日前後に、**盛装**して両親とともに近所の神社や寺にお参りを
　とし　　がつ　にちぜん ご　　せいそう　　　　りょうしん　　　　　　きんじょ　じんじゃ　てら　　まい
する。そこで、縁起が良いとされる「千歳飴」を買ったりもする。なにせ
　　　　　　　　えん ぎ　よ　　　　　　　　ち とせあめ　　か
この**紅白模様**の細長い飴を食べると1000歳まで長生きできるのだ。
　こうはくも よう　　ほそなが　あめ　た　　　　　　　　せんさい　　　ながい

2. *Shichi-go-san*: Childhood Milestones

Relief when the child reaches the age of seven in good health

Even if a child survives infancy, the worries of parents do not end there. Indeed, an infant's development was considered so risky that there's a saying "Children are in the hands of the gods until the age of seven." In Japan it became popular to hold ceremonies at the ages of three, five, and seven to pray for the safe growth of a child, a practice known as *shichi-go-san* (7–5–3). There are variations in different regions, but on or around November 15, girls aged three or seven, and boys aged three or five are dressed up and go with their parents to visit a shrine or temple. There they buy long sticks of red and white candy called *chitose-ame* (1,000-year candy), which is considered lucky and said to enable them to live for a thousand years.

☐ 乳児期 infancy
☐ 乗り切る survive
☐ 乳幼児 infant
☐ 成育 development
☐ 奇数年齢 odd-numbered ages
☐ 目安 indication
☐ 普及する become popular
☐ 盛装する dress up
☐ 紅白模様 red-and-white pattern

千歳飴を持つ子供
A child holding *chitose-ame*

3. 成人

13

自立した大人として認められる儀式

　子供が無事に育てば、次は「大人として独り立ちできるように」と願うのも当然の親心。そして社会的に一人前と見なされる年齢に達したとき、感謝と将来へ祝福や期待を込めて盛大かつ厳粛に行うのが成人の儀式である。平均寿命が40歳台だった昔の日本（といっても1920年代まで続いた）では、男の子が15歳前後になると冠を着ける「加冠式」あるいは「元服式」を行い、女の子は13歳前後で「十三祝い」を行った。この儀式を経ることで外見的にも大人の仲間入りをし、侍で成人した場合は翌年から一人前の「扶持(給与)」をもらえた。

　2022年から成人年齢が18歳に引き下げられた。しかし、ほとんどの地方自治体では20歳を迎えた年度の1月第2月曜に「成人式」を催す。帰省しやすい夏のお盆に行う地方もある。

　世界には民族ごとにいろいろな成人への通過儀礼があることはよく知られているが、全国一斉にこうしたイベントを行うのは日本くらいのものだろう。

「二十歳のつどい」に出席する成人

Adults attending a "gathering of twenty-year-olds"

3. Coming of Age

Ceremony at which children are recognized as independent adults

Any parent, having successfully raised their child, will next hope to see them able to stand on their own feet as an adult. The Coming-of-Age ceremony held when they reach the age at which society considers them adult is a grand and solemn occasion filled with thanks as well as blessings and hopes for the future. In the past, when the average life expectancy in Japan was age forty (which was actually the case up to 1920), a *kakanshiki* (crowning ceremony, to fit boys with a traditional cap) or *genpukushiki* (coming-of-age ceremony) was held for boys aged around fifteen years, while the *jūsan iwai* (thirteen celebration) was held for girls around age thirteen. By going through these ceremonies, children joined the ranks of adults, and a samurai coming of age would receive his own stipend (salary) the following year.

In 2022, the age of adulthood was lowered to eighteen. However, most local governments still hold a coming-of-age ceremony on the second Monday in January for those who turned twenty during the past year.

Various rites of passage for coming of age in different countries around the world are well known, but it's possible that Japan is the only country that stages events nationwide.

□自立した independent

□育てる raise

□独り立ちする stand on one's own feet

□感謝 thanks

□祝福 blessing

□期待 hope

□盛大に grand

□厳粛に solemn

□成人の儀式 Coming-of-Age ceremony

□平均寿命 average life expectancy

□大人の仲間入りをする join the ranks of adults

□扶持 stipend

□地方自治体 local government

□通過儀礼 rites of passage

□全国一斉に nationwide

□イベントを行う stage events

成人としての権利と義務

　現代の日本では18歳から選挙権が与えられるが、飲酒・喫煙、馬券の購入（学生を除く）が認められるのは20歳から。ちなみに14歳になって罪を犯すと刑事責任を負う。15歳だと自分の意思で他人の養子になったり、遺言をすることができる。16歳になると二輪免許が取得できる。そして18歳になると普通自動車の免許が取得でき、男女とも両親の同意があれば結婚できる。なぜかパチンコ店への入店もできるようになる。つまり、18歳でいきなり大人として扱うのでなく、少年期から徐々に社会的に受け入れられるようになっている。

Rights and duties as an adult

Nowadays in Japan, once you turn eighteen you are given the right to vote, and once you turn twenty you are allowed to drink, smoke, and also bet on horse races (unless you are a student). Incidentally, fourteen is the age from which you are held criminally responsible. From fifteen you can choose to be adopted into another family, and to make your own will. From sixteen you can get a motorbike license. From eighteen you can get a driving license, and marry with their parents' permission. For some reason you can also go into a *pachinko* parlor. In other words, it is not as though you suddenly become an adult at age eighteen, as you are gradually accepted into society during your teens.

☐ 選挙権 right to vote

☐ 飲酒 drink

☐ 喫煙 smoke

☐ 馬券を購入する bet on horse a race

☐ 刑事責任を負う be held criminally responsible

☐ 意思 will

☐ 普通自動車の免許 driving license

☐ 同意 permission

☐ なぜか for some reason

☐ つまり in other words

☐ 徐々に gradually

じんせい

4. 賀寿
が じゅ

14

ややこしい「十干 十二支」の思想
じっかんじゅう に し   し そう

　前章「正月」の年男・年女で説明したように、自分が生まれた年によっ
て「干支」があり象徴となる動物がある。そして12年ごとに自分の干支が
巡ってくる。しかし、厳密にいうと自分の生まれた年の干支は60年サイク
ルである。これは陰陽五行の考え方に基づくもので、「五行＝5つの元素＝
木・火・土・金・水」のそれぞれにも「干＝兄＝陽」と「支＝弟＝陰」があ
るという意味で、「木の兄」「木の弟」「火の兄」などとなり、全部で10通り
になる。ややこしいのはこの10通り（10の順序）にそれぞれ固有の名前がつ
くことである。それが「甲・乙・丙・丁・戊・己・庚・辛・壬・癸」の「十
干」である。この「十干」と「十二支」を組み合わせて、その年の呼び方
が決まり、最初に来るのは「きのえ（甲）のネズミ（子）年」で「甲子＝きのえ
ね」で次が「乙丑＝きのとうし」。以下、10通
りと12通りを組み合わせながら進むのだから
全部で60通り、つまり60年かけて暦が一巡
することになる。

陰陽五行説と十干
いんようごぎょうせつ　じっかん

Yin-yang, Five Elements Theory
and *Jikkan*

五行 ごぎょう	十干 じっかん		陰陽 いんよう
木 き	甲 きのえ	（木の兄） き え	陽 よう
	乙 きのと	（木の弟） き と	陰 いん
火 ひ	丙 ひのえ	（火の兄） ひ え	陽 よう
	丁 ひのと	（火の弟） ひ と	陰 いん
土 つち	戊 つちのえ	（土の兄） つち え	陽 よう
	己 つちのと	（土の弟） つち と	陰 いん
金 か（ね）	庚 かのえ	（金の兄） か え	陽 よう
	辛 かのと	（金の弟） か と	陰 いん
水 みず	壬 みずのえ	（水の兄） みず え	陽 よう
	癸 みずのと	（水の弟） みず と	陰 いん

4. Long-life Celebrations

The complex ideology of the Sexagenary Cycle

As explained earlier, under the Oriental zodiac everyone's year of birth is symbolically represented by a particular animal that comes around every twelve years. These are known as the Twelve Earthly Branches. However, strictly speaking, your particular birth year animal only comes round once every sixty years. This is based on the doctrine of yin yang and the five elements, with the five elements being wood, fire, earth, metal and water, which are further categorized as yin and yang, giving yang wood and yin wood, yang fire and yin fire, and so on for a total of ten. What is complex about these is that each has its own name: 甲 *kō*, 乙 *otsu*, 丙 *hei*, 丁 *tei*, 戊 *bo*, 己 *ki*, 庚 *kō*, 辛 *shin*, 壬 *jin*, and 癸 *ki*. These are known as the Ten Heavenly Stems, which are combined with the Twelve Earthly Branches to determine the name of a particular year, starting with yang wood, or *kō*, and the animal Rat, or *shi*, followed by yin wood Ox, and so on. If you continue to thus combine the Ten Heavenly Stems with the Twelve Earthly branches, you eventually get a total of sixty distinct animal-element years, occurring over a period of sixty calendar years.

じっかんじゅう に し
十干十二支

Ten Heavenly Stems, Twelve Earthly Branches

じっかん 十干	じゅう に し 十二支
きのえ 甲	ね 子
きのと 乙	うし 丑
ひのえ 丙	とら 寅
ひのと 丁	う 卯
つちのえ 戊	たつ 辰
つちのと 己	み 巳
かのえ 庚	うま 午
かのと 辛	ひつじ 未
みずのえ 壬	さる 申
みずのと 癸	とり 酉
きのえ 甲	いぬ 戌
きのと 乙	い 亥
ひのえ 丙	ね 子
ひのと 丁	うし 丑
つちのえ 戊	とら 寅
つちのと 己	う 卯
かのえ 庚	たつ 辰
かのえ 庚	み 巳
かのと 辛	うま 午
みずのえ 壬	ひつじ 未
みずのと 癸	さる 申
きのえ 甲	とり 酉
きのと 乙	いぬ 戌
ひのえ 丙	い 亥
⋮	⋮

□象徴 symbol

□巡ってくる come around

□厳密にいうと strictly speaking

□元素 element

□ややこしいのは what is complex about these is

□固有の own

□十干 Ten Heavenly Stems

□十二支 Twelve Earthly Branches

□一巡する complete a cycle

「赤いちゃんちゃんこ」を着る還暦

　以上の説明で察しがつくと思うが、人生を何とか生き抜いて、自分の生まれた年が数え年61歳で巡ってくるというのは、祝うべき長寿(賀寿)ということになる。それは良いとしても、なぜその祝いに赤い頭巾、赤いちゃんちゃんこを着て、赤い座布団に座らされるのかがわかりにくい。暦がひと巡りすることは生まれた赤ん坊に戻ること(本卦還り)だという考え方はある。そこで「赤ちゃん＝赤ちゃんちゃんこ」と洒落たのだという説がある。また赤色は、風水的に魔よけの強い色だからとの説もある。孔子は、この年齢くらいになったら他人の意見に従えという意味で60歳を「耳順」と呼んだ。赤づくしなんて由来の知れぬ悪趣味だと怒るのは大人気ないらしい。

還暦の祝い
(赤い頭巾とちゃんちゃんこ)
Celebrating *Kanreki*
(Red Cap and Vest [*Chanchanko*])

Age 60: *Kanreki* and wearing an *akachanchanko* red padded vest

As may be deduced from the above explanation, if you somehow survive until your sixty-first year, your birth year animal will be repeated, and this longevity is something to be celebrated. Why, then, are you expected to celebrate such an auspicious occasion by wearing a red headscarf or padded vest and sitting on a red cushion? One theory is that by completing the sixty-year cycle (the literal meaning of *kanreki*) and returning to your birth year, you are returning to being a baby, which gives rise to some witty word play. The word for baby in Japanese is 赤ちゃん *akachan*, where 赤 means "red," and ちゃん doubled gives you *chanchan*, the beginning of the word *chanchanko* which is a Japanese-style padded vest. Another theory holds that according to feng shui, red is a strong color that protects against evil. Confucius called the age of sixty "obedient ears" since at that age you should be able to take other people's opinion in your stride—in other words, complaining that wearing red is a vulgar custom of unknown origins is really beneath you at that age.

☐ 察しがつく deduce
☐ 頭巾 headscarf
☐ ちゃんちゃんこ padded vest
☐ 本卦還り reaching age of 60, second children
☐ 洒落る give rise to some witty word play
☐ 風水 feng shui
☐ 魔よけ protect against evil
☐ 孔子 Confucius
☐ 耳順 obedient ears
☐ 赤づくし exhaustive collection of red
☐ 由来の知れぬ unknown origin
☐ 悪趣味 bad taste
☐ 大人気ない immature

祝うべき長寿「賀寿」いろいろ

　60歳の還暦まで生きることが例外的な祝い事だと考えられたのに、それ以上生きるとなると、周囲も唖然としながらも何とか寿ぐべき呼び方なり儀式なりを用意しなくてはと思っただろう。以下、怪しいものも含めて「賀寿」一覧である（すべて数え年）。

66歳＝緑寿（2002年に日本百貨店協会が提唱。緑々寿）

70歳＝古希（杜甫の詩「人生七十古来稀」より）

77歳＝喜寿（七を3つ重ねて書くと㐂＝喜の草書体）

80歳＝傘寿（縦に八十を書くと仐＝傘の略字）

81歳＝半寿（半の字を分解すると八十一）

88歳＝米寿（米の字を分解すると八十八）

90歳＝卒寿（縦に九十を書くと卆＝卒の略字）

99歳＝白寿（百引く一＝99）

100歳＝百寿

108歳＝茶寿（草冠は ＋＋ でその下は八十八だから）

……この上もまだあって、2度目の還暦を迎えたら

120歳＝大還暦もあるが、もういいだろう。

Some particular ages to celebrate

Although it was considered exceptionally auspicious to live until the age of sixty and anything beyond that was quite amazing, people probably also thought they should prepare some specific celebrations just in case. Below is a list of all the long-life celebrations, including the more dubious ones (all given in the traditional Japanese system of being considered one year old at birth, with one year added at every New Year).

Age 66 is *rokuju* ("green celebration," introduced by the Japan Department Store Association in 2002); age 70 is *koki* (from a line by the poet Du Fu, "Men seldom live to be seventy"); age 77 is *kiju* ("felicitous celebration"—writing the number 7 three times in cursive script brings good luck); age 80 is *sanju* ("umbrella celebration"—writing the number 80 in kanji in vertical script produces a simplified version of the kanji for "umbrella"); age 81 is *hanju* ("half celebration"—putting the elements of the three kanji used in the number 81 together produces the kanji for "half"); age 88 is *beiju* ("rice celebration"—putting the elements of the three kanji used in the number 88 together produces the kanji for "rice"); age 90 is *sotsuju* (a simplified version of the kanji *sotsu* can read as a combination of nine and ten); age 99 is *hakuju* ("white celebration"—the kanji for "white" lacks one stroke that would make it the kanji for "hundred"); age 100 is *hyakuju* ("hundred celebration"); age 108 is *chaju* ("tea celebration"—the kanji for "tea" is made up of the five kanji used to write 10, 10, and 88). There are still more after this, and if you reach your second *kanreki* at the age of 120, it is called *daikanreki*, or "great *kanreki*"—but that's enough, surely!

☐ 唖然 quite amazing
☐ 寿ぐ celebrate
☐ 怪しい dubious
☐ 一欄 list
☐ 提唱する introduce
☐ 草書体 cursive script
☐ 縦の vertical
☐ 略字 simplified version of kanji
☐ 草冠：⁺⁺, ⁺⁺, one of kanji radicals

5. 厄年

15

男42歳、女33歳は要注意の年齢

　年齢を重ねることはめでたいとは限らない。人生には災厄が待ち構えている危険な年齢もあるというのが「厄年」である。一般に知られているのは、男42歳、女33歳(いずれも数え年)の「大厄」で、中程度だと男25歳と61歳(還暦も厄年！)、女19歳と37歳がそれに当たる。そしてこれらの厄年の1年前は「前厄」、1年後は「後厄」と呼んでやはり注意を要する年齢ということになっている。そして「厄年」を迎える人は寺社でお払い(厄除け)をしてもらい、体調を気遣い、行動を自重するべきだとされる。やっかいなのは当人だけでなく、その家族にも災厄が及ぶことがあるという。

　なぜ、この年齢が厄年なのかを説明できる理由はない。42が「死に」で33が「散々」に通じるなどというのは愚にもつかない。ただ、経験的に言えるのは、働き盛りで無理を重ねやすい年齢であるとか、体調が変化する年齢だからというのは納得できる。人生ドライブのシフトチェンジを促すのが「厄払い」だともいえる。だから現代でも、「厄年」を気遣う人は少なくない。世界各地にも似たような厄年の考え方、厄払いの儀式があるという。

5. *Yakudoshi*: Unlucky Years

The ages 42 for men and 33 for women require caution

Adding on the years is not always something to be celebrated. There are also danger years that are said to be potentially calamitous, called *yakudoshi*, or unlucky years. The main ones that everyone knows about are the ages 42 for men and 33 for women (both in the traditional Japanese way of calculating age), but there are also the moderately unlucky years of 25 and 61 for men (*kanreki* is also an unlucky year for them!), and 19 and 37 for women. The years before and after a *yakudoshi* also require vigilance. Those approaching a *yakudoshi* should visit a temple or shrine to ward off the misfortune, take care of their physical health, and act prudently. It is not only the person themselves who is affected, but the calamity may befall his whole family.

There are no reasons to explain why these ages are *yakudoshi*. Some say that 42 is homophonous with *shini* or "die," and 33 with *sanzan* or "merciless," but this is nonsense. More convincing, however, is the suggestion that they are ages when one is in the prime of one's working life and it is easy to overdo things, or when physical changes in the body. It is also said that the need to ward off misfortune is a way of telling us that it's time for a gear change occur in our journey of life. Even nowadays, therefore, there are many people who pay attention to *yakudoshi*. Apparently there are similar unlucky years and ceremonies to dispel misfortune in countries all around the world.

□ 年齢を重ねること adding on the years
□ 注意 vigilance
□ お払いをする ward off the misfortune
□ 体調 physical health
□ 気遣う take care of
□ 自重する act prudently
□ 当人 person themselves
□ 災厄 calamity
□ 及ぶ befall
□ 散々な merciless
□ 愚にもつかない nonsense
□ 働き盛り prime of one's working life
□ 無理を重ねやすい easy to overdo things
□ 体調が変化する physical changes in one's body
□ 現代でも even nowadays
□ 気遣う pay attention to
□ 世界各地に in countries all around the world
□ 儀式 ceremony

3

婚礼・葬儀・宗教
Weddings, Funerals, and Religion

1. 婚約まで

16

結婚を急がない、結婚を選ばない時代に

結婚は家の存続、労働力確保の手段でもあった昔の日本では、適齢期になれば結婚するのが当然のことだった。しかし現代では個人の意思で決めるものとなり、結婚を急がないあるいは結婚を選択しない人も増えている。平均的な結婚年齢は、1970年には夫が27.6歳、妻が24.6歳だったものが2018年には31.2歳と29.6歳になり「晩婚化」傾向が顕著である（厚生労働省資料）。適齢になっても結婚していない「未婚率」でみると、1930年の25～29歳の男性の未婚率は28.7%、女性が8.5%だったものが、2015年には男性が72.7%、女性が61.3%にもなっている（国勢調査資料）。

「仲人」を立てて「お見合い」をする

当人たちの意思で結婚を決めるのが主流になる以前は、「仲人」を立てて「お見合い」をすることが普通だった。仲人は職場の上司や一族の長老や近所の世話好きなどで、男女双方の家を行き来し、たがいの紹介文に写真などを添えた「釣書」を交わして話をまとめ、当人たちを引き合わせる「お見合い」の場を設けた。

1. Courtship and Engagement

An age when people choose not to rush into marriage, or not to marry at all

In the past, when marriage was a means of continuing family lines and securing a supply of labor, getting married upon reaching the appropriate age was a matter of course. These days, however, people can decide for themselves and increasingly they are choosing not to rush into marriage, or even not to marry at all. The average age upon marriage in 1970 was 27.6 for men and 24.6 for women, but in 2018 it was 32.2 and 29.6 respectively, showing a marked trend for marrying later (figures from the Ministry of Health, Labour and Welfare). If we look at the rate of those unmarried despite having reached marriageable age, in 1930 28.7% of men and 8.5% of women between the ages of 25–29 remained unmarried, while in 2015 the rate was 72.7% of men and 61.3% of women respectively (figures from national population censuses).

□存続 contine (to exist)
□労働力 supply of labor
□手段 mean
□適齢期 appropriate age
□当然のこと matter of course
□晩婚 marrying later
□傾向が顕著である show a marked trend
□厚生労働省 Ministry of Health, Labour and Welfare
□未婚 unmarried
□国勢調査 national population censuses

The *nakōdo* (go-between) and *omiai* (meeting prospective marriage partners)

Before it became the norm for people to choose their own marriage partners, it was customary to appoint a go-between (*nakōdo*) who would introduce suitable candidates (*omiai*). The go-between was one's boss, a clan elder, or an obliging neighbor, who would mediate between both sides, exchanging the "personal resumes" with attached photos and negotiating the details, and arranging the place where the *omiai* would be held to bring both parties together.

□主流になる become the norm
□仲人 go-between
□立てる appoint
□一族の長老 clan elder
□近所の世話好き obliging neighbor
□釣書 personal resume
□当人たちを引き合わせる bring both parties together

お見合いの場は、女性側の家であったり演劇や食事のできる場所だったりとさまざま。当人たちとその両親、仲人が立ち会って紹介し合った後、当人たちだけでうちとける時間を作る。気にいるか否かの意思表示として、「出された茶菓に手をつける」あるいは「男性が自分の扇を置いて帰る」とOKで、そうでなければNOといった約束事を設ける場合もあるが、一般的には後日、仲人にその意思を伝えた。

「婚約」に鰹節やスルメや昆布？

結婚に先立って「婚約」の儀式をする習慣は多くの国にある。日本では、新婦の家に仲人と新郎とその両親が出向いて、「帯料」と書いたお金と記念の品々を贈る。両方の家が結ばれることを了承するこの儀式を「結納」、贈られるお金は「結納金」、品々は「結納品」と呼ぶ。この「結納金」は新婦が嫁入りの際に「持参金」とする場合もある。

日本的なのは「結納品」の品々である。すべて縁起の良い語呂合わせで組み合わされる。たとえば鰹節は「勝つ男」で男性の頼もしさを、長期保存できるスルメは「寿留女」で末永い幸せを、昆布は「子生婦」で子孫繁栄を、扇は開いた形から「末広がり」の繁栄を…といった具合。ただし関東と関西では内容が違うものもある。

The *omiai* could be held in a variety of places, such as the prospective bride's home, at the theater, or somewhere where a meal could be provided. After the go-between had introduced the prospective couple and their parents, the two would be given time alone to break the ice. Partaking of the refreshments served, or in the man's case leaving his personal fan behind, were ways of signaling interest, or sometimes conventions were established to indicate otherwise, but generally speaking the intentions were communicated by the go-between the following day.

An engagement sealed by dried bonito, dried squid, and kelp?

Ceremonies to seal an engagement ahead of marriage are held in many countries. In Japan, the go-between, the groom and his parents proceed to the bride's home with money in an envelope marked *obiryō* (betrothal money) and other gifts to mark the occasion. This ceremonial exchange of betrothal gifts, called *yuinō*, marks the joining together of the two families. The money given is called *yuinōkin* and other items are called *yuinōhin*. This betrothal money is sometimes given as a dowry on the occasion of the marriage.

What is particularly Japanese about the betrothal gifts are the items given. These are all based on auspicious wordplay. For example, dried bonito is *katsuo-bushi*, a homophone for 勝つ男, indicating the man's dependability; dried squid is *surume*, a homophone for 寿留女, indicating a wish for many years of happiness for the woman; and kelp is *konbu*, a homophone for 子生婦, indicating a desire for numerous offspring; and an open fan indicates a desire for increasing prosperity over the years. However, the details differ between eastern and western Japan.

□ うちとける break the ice
□ 茶菓 refreshments
□ 扇 fan
□ 約束事 convention
□ 一般的には generally speaking
□ 後日 following day
□ 意思 intention

□ 婚約 engagement, betrothal
□ 新婦 bride
□ 新郎 groom
□ 帯料 betrothal money
□ 持参金 dowry
□ 語呂合わせ wordplay
□ 鰹節 dried bonito
□ 頼もしさ dependability
□ スルメ dried squid
□ 昆布 kelp
□ 子孫繁栄 numerous offspring
□ 末広がり spreading out like an open fan
□ 繁栄 prosperity

2.結婚式と披露宴

17

「三々九度」の盃を交わすだけの誓い

　中世までの日本では結婚式はなかった。男性が女性のところに通う「通い婚」が普通であり、周囲にそのことを知らせる適当な時期に「**披露宴**」を行っていた。江戸時代から20世紀半ば(戦前)までは、**新郎**の家で双方の家族やゆかりのある人などを招き、近所の主婦などが世話して宴を設ける「人前式」が普通だった。**結婚の誓い**も、新郎新婦が大小3組の酒盃をそれぞれ3回にわけて(合計9回)飲む「三々九度」の儀式だけだった。

多様化した結婚式

　現代の日本の結婚式は多様である。「**人前式**」以外にも「神前式」、「仏前式」、「キリスト教式」などがある。「神前式」のルーツは1900年の大正天皇の結婚式、「キリスト教式」のルーツは1876年の新島襄と八重の結婚式といわれる。**結婚雑誌**「ゼクシィ」の**調査**(2009年)によると、カップルの99%は仲人を立てず、60.4%がキリスト教式(2位は人前式20.4%、3位神前式17%)だった。**ちなみに**日本のキリスト教信者は300万人に過ぎないが、キリスト教式の挙式が**カッコイイ**と考える人が多いのだ。

2. The Wedding Ceremony and Reception

Sansankudo: exchanging nuptial cups

Wedding ceremonies were not held in Japan until the Middle Ages. The norm was for men to visit their wives' homes in "commuter marriages," and at the appropriate time a reception was held to inform everyone of this. From the Edo period until the mid-twentieth century (prewar), the norm was for the families and relatives of both sides to be invited to the groom's home for a banquet prepared by local housewives. The wedding oath was a simple ritual known as *sansankudo*, in which a stack of three sake cups of different sizes were filled three times (a total of nine cups), each shared by the couple.

A variety of wedding ceremonies

These days there are many different types of weddings held in Japan. In addition to non-religious ceremonies, there are also Shinto weddings, Buddhist weddings, and Christian weddings. Shinto weddings are said to have their roots in the marriage of Emperor Taisho in 1900, and Christian ceremonies in that of Joseph Hardy Neesima to his wife Yae. According to a survey by the wedding magazine *Zexy* (2009), 99% of couples didn't use a go-between, 60.4% had a Christian ceremony (in second place was a secular ceremony at 20.4%, and a Shinto ceremony in third place at 17%). Incidentally, there are fewer than three million Christians in Japan, but many people think it's cool to hold a Christian-style ceremony.

□普通 norm
□適当な appropriate
□披露宴 reception
□新郎 groom
□ゆかりのある人 relatives
□宴 banquet
□結婚の誓い wedding oath
□酒盃 sake cup

□人前式 non-religious ceremonies, secular ceremony
□結婚雑誌 wedding magazine
□調査 survey
□ちなみに incidentally
□カッコイイ cool

「お色直し」と「引き出物」

　披露宴が華やかなものになるのは1960年代の高度成長期からである。その演出の中で日本的なのは「お色直し」と「引き出物」かもしれない。「お色直し」は、本来、花嫁が礼服である白無垢や打掛けから、色のついた比較的地味な着物に着替え、少しでも早く嫁いだ家で働くことを示すものだった。しかしいつの間にかウェディングドレスから豪華な着物（あるいはその逆）に着替えて見せるショーになり、花婿まで「お色直し」するようになってきた。また「引き出物」は、平安時代に貴族が祝い事の際に馬を庭先に引き出して賓客に贈呈したのがルーツだった。それが現代になって食器セットなどの記念品を参加者に贈呈するものになり、さらには自由なものを選べるカタログ方式になっている。

花嫁衣裳
（左：白無垢・綿帽子、右：色打ち掛け・角隠し）

Bridal Gowns
(L: White Kimono with Cotton Headpiece,
R: Colorful Kimono Overcoat and *Tsuno Kakushi* Headpiece)

O-ironaoshi and *hikidemono*

It was only since the period of rapid economic growth in the 1960s that the wedding reception became a showy affair. The most Japanese elements of the proceedings are probably the *o-ironaoshi,* the bride's change of outfit, and *hikidemono,* the gifts given to guests to take home with them. Originally, the bride would change from the all-white kimono and elaborate bridal robe worn for the ceremony into a relatively simple but colored kimono to indicate her eagerness to get to work in the marital home. However, at some point this became a show of changing from a Western-style wedding dress into a sumptuous kimono (or sometimes the other way round), and even the bridegrooms have got in on the act now. The *hikidemono* has its roots in celebrations held by court nobles during the Heian period, when a horse would be brought out into the garden and presented to the guest of honor. Nowadays this has become an item of food or crockery given to guests as a memento, and sometimes even a catalogue from which guests can choose their own gift.

□華やかな showy
□高度成長 rapid economic growth
□本来 originally
□花嫁 bride
□白無垢 all-white kimono
□打掛け robe
□比較的 relatively
□嫁いだ家 marital home
□豪華な sumptuous
□貴族 court nobles
□賓客 guest of honor
□贈呈する present
□食器セット crockery
□記念品 memento

3.式日／六曜
しきじつ　ろくよう

18

何かを行うのに良い日、悪い日
なに　おこな　よ　ひ　わる　ひ

　婚礼などの慶事や、葬式などの弔事など、重要な儀式を行う日を式日という。その際に目安になるのが、「先勝」「友引」「大安」「仏滅」などその日ごとに替わる六種類の「六曜」である。元は中国の陰陽道だというもののはっきりしないが1ヵ月を5週間×6日とし、その時の星回りから戦争や儀式の進め方を決めた。そして「結婚式は大安に」、「葬式は友引を避ける」などといわれるようになったのは、六曜ごとに意味があるからだ。

　先勝（せんしょう・さきがち）：何事も先んじた方が良い。午前中が吉で午後が凶。

　友引（ともびき）：友を引き込むことから凶事は避ける。勝負事なら引き分けになる。

　先負（せんぶ・さきまけ）：急ぐと失敗する。午前中は凶で午後からが吉。

　仏滅（ぶつめつ）：仏が滅した大凶の日。祝い事や勝負事は避ける。

　大安（たいあん・だいあん）：最高に吉の日。ただしすぐ凶に転じやすいので要注意。

　赤口（しゃっこう・せきぐち）：凶の日だが正午前後2時間は吉。火や血に注意。

Auspicious and Unlucky Days

Good and bad days to hold an event

The days on which important ceremonies should be held, whether felicitous occasions such as weddings or unfortunate occasions such as funerals, are called *shikijitsu*. These are determined by the cycle of six lucky and unlucky days known as *rokuyō*. It's not clear whether or not this is originally from the Chinese doctrine of yin yang, but in one month there are thought to be five cycles of six days which determined how to proceed with, say, a war, or a ceremony. Also, each of these days has its own particular meaning, which is why it is said, for example, that weddings should be held on *taian* days, and that funerals should not be held on *tomobiki* days.

□婚礼 wedding
□慶事 felicitous occasion
□葬式 funeral
□弔事 unfortunate occasion
□進め方 how to proceed
□午前 morning
□午後 afternoon
□勝負事 competitive event
□引き分け draw
□失敗 failure
□大凶の日 unluckiest day
□祝い事 celebrations
□勝負事 competitive events
□血 blood

 Senshō (or *sakigachi*): whatever you do, better do it early. The morning is lucky, afternoon unlucky.

 Tomobiki: a day when your luck affects other people, so should be avoided for unfortunate occasions. In the case of competitive events, the result will be a draw.

 Senbu (or *sakimake*): haste will end in failure. Mornings are unlucky, afternoons lucky.

 Butsumetsu: the day of Buddha's death, the unluckiest day. Celebrations and competitive events should be avoided.

 Taian (or *daian*): the luckiest day, although good luck can easily change to bad luck, so care is needed.

 Shakkō (or *sekiguchi*): an unlucky day, although the two hours around noon are lucky. Beware of fire and blood.

4. 葬儀

19

仏教式が圧倒的に多い理由

人の誕生と死は、人の心を厳粛にする。世界各地にはさまざまな弔いの儀式があるが、日本では江戸時代以降、仏教式で行われることが多い。これは、集落の住民（信徒）を各宗派の寺（檀家寺）に管理させる「寺請制度」が徹底されたからだ。寺が共同体の冠婚葬祭行事の執行役と戸籍係を兼ねたようなもので、農作業などでの相互扶助の仕組みとも一体になっていた。制度がなくなった現代でも葬儀は仏教式で行われることが多い。

葬儀の順序

死者が出ると僧侶を招いて読経してもらい、清めた遺体を棺に納め、近親のものたちが香を絶やさぬよう一晩中見守る「通夜」が行われる。日取り（式日）を見ながら翌日あるいは翌々日には、会葬者が「香典」を持って集まり、「告別式」が行われ、火葬（一部の地域は土葬）した遺骨を墓に納める。地域によっては火葬の後に告別式を行うところもある。その順序や作法は宗派ごと、地域ごとで些細な違いがある。

死者を北の方角に頭を向けて安置する「北枕」とか枕頭の屏風を逆さに立てる「逆さ屏風」、お棺に入れる「六文銭」や「わらじ」、火葬場に向かう出棺時の「茶碗割り」、信徒仲間による「かねたたき」、葬礼から帰った人にかける「清めの塩」等々は今も踏襲されることが多い。

---

4. Funerals

Why the vast majority of funerals are Buddhist

Births and deaths are occasions that put people in a solemn frame of mind. There are various types of funeral services around the world, but in Japan the Buddhist service has been the most common since the Edo period. This is because there was a strictly enforced system to ensure that everyone in the community (parishioners) was registered to a Buddhist temple, regardless of sect. The temples were effectively community managers, overseeing coming-of-age, marriage, burial, and other ceremonial occasions as well as the family registers, so they also came to serve as a mutual aid organization for farm work. Even now, when that system no longer exists, many people hold a Buddhist service for funerals.

The procedure in funerals

When someone dies, a priest is summoned to chant sutras, the cleansed body is placed in the coffin, and the immediate family holds a wake keeping incense burning throughout the night. Over the next day or two until the day appointed for the funeral, mourners gather bringing a monetary funeral offering (literally, "incense money"), then the "farewell ceremony" is held, and the bones from the cremation are placed in the tomb (in some regions burials are held). Depending on the area, the farewell ceremony is held after the cremation. The exact procedures and etiquette varies according to the sect and region.

Customs that are often observed even now include the "north pillow," in which the body is placed with the head facing north, the "upside-down screen," in which the folding screen placed at the bedside is stood upside down, placing six one-*mon* coins and some straw sandals in the coffin, breaking a bowl when the body leaves for the crematorium, beating the gong by mourners, throwing salt over those returning from the funeral to purify them.

- □ 誕生 birth
- □ 厳粛に solemn
- □ 弔い fureral
- □ 冠婚葬祭行事 coming-of-age, marriage, burial, and other ceremonial occasions
- □ 戸籍 family register
- □ 農作業 farm work
- □ 相互扶助の仕組み mutual aid organization

- □ 棺 coffin
- □ 香 incense
- □ 一晩中 throughout the night
- □ 通夜 wake
- □ 会葬者 mourner
- □ 香典 monetary funeral offering
- □ 告別式 farewell ceremony
- □ 火葬 cremation
- □ 土葬 burial
- □ 順序 procedure
- □ 作法 etiquette
- □ 屏風 folding screen
- □ わらじ straw sandal
- □ 火葬場 crematorium
- □ 今も踏襲される be observed even now

　これら一連の行事ごとに僧侶（および信徒）による読経が行われる。また死んで仏の弟子になったという意味で、仏教的な「戒名（または法名）」を僧侶が付けたりする。

死後の仏事（法事）

　葬礼は死後も続く。追悼のために「法要」とよばれる仏教儀式が月日の区切りごとに行われる。死んで7日目が「初七日」で、以後7日ごとに行われるが大きな節目は「四十九日（7×7日目）」。この日を境に死者の霊魂が仏の住む浄土に行く。墓への納骨や位牌を仏壇に納める。以後は、「百か日」「一周忌（1年目）」「三回忌」「七回忌」「十三回忌」「三十三回忌」などと続く。大きな法要のときは僧侶による読経、墓参、遺族・親族による会食などを行う。

仏事に使う数珠と袋

Buddhist rosary and a bag used for Buddhist ceremonies

オリジナルな自由葬

　最近の日本では、こうしたしきたりに縛られない「自由葬」を希望する人が増えている。無宗教で故人を「しのぶ会」だけにする。遺骨を墓に入れず散骨する。戒名をつけない。法要を最小限に省略する。墓も仏壇もいらない。生前に知人・友人を招いて「生前葬」をする等々、遺族にも負担にならず、生前の生き方も尊重するオリジナルな「弔われ方」を望んでいる。

During all these procedures, a priest chants sutras. Also, the priest confers a posthumous name to signify that the deceased has now become a disciple of Buddha.

□読経する chant sutras
□弟子 disciple
□戒名 posthumous name

Memorial services held after death

A number of services are held following a death. Buddhist services for mourning, called *hōyō*, are held at certain intervals over time. The seventh day after death is *shonanuka*, and every seventh day after that is also observed until the main turning point at the forty-ninth day (7 x 7 days). This is the point at which the deceased's soul goes to the Pure Land where Buddha resides. The ashes are interred and the memorial tablet is placed on the family altar. After this, other specified dates are the hundredth day, the one-year anniversary, the second anniversary, the sixth anniversary, the twelfth anniversary, the thirty-second anniversary, and so on. On these major dates, a priest chants sutras, and the bereaved family and relatives visit the grave and have dinner together.

□区切り interval
□節目 turning point
□霊魂 soul
□浄土 Pure Land
□墓への納骨 interring the ashes
□位牌 memorial tablet
□仏壇 family altar
□遺族 bereaved family
□親族 relative

Original free-form funerals

Recently, more and more Japanese people have been holding a "free-form" funeral unconstricted by these traditional practices, and simply hold a non-religious memorial service for the deceased. Instead of interring the ashes, they scatter them; they do not confer a posthumous Buddhist name; they keep the number of subsequent mourning dates to a minimum; and there is no grave or memorial tablet. Some people opt to invite their friends and acquaintances to a "living funeral" while they are still alive, in an original form of mourning that respects their lifestyle and avoids being a burden on their families.

□自由葬 free form funeral
□散骨する scatter the ashes
□法要 subsequent mourning date
□知人 acquaintance
□生前葬 living funeral
□負担 burden
□生き方 lifestyle

5. 神と仏

20

今も昔も神と仏が混在する国

日本人は宗教的に厳格でないといわれる。たしかに生まれた時は神社に「お宮参り」に行き、結婚式はキリスト教式で行い、死んだら仏教で弔う。お正月には神棚に向かい、お盆には仏壇に手を合わせ、バレンタインやクリスマスにはスイーツを買い求める。宗教を信じない無宗教ではなく、つごうに合わせて使い分けている。

神社や寺院にしても、敷地の一角に「なんとか稲荷」や「天神様」などがあったりするのだから、厳格な一神教の文化で育った外国人にはわかりにくい。

古来、たくさんの神々が住む国だった

日本(アイヌと琉球を除く)の「国造り」伝説(『古事記』『日本書紀』など)では、天の神々の末裔であるイザナギ・イザナミの夫婦神が日本列島を生み、その子孫のアマテラスオオミカミやスサノオらによるいろんな事件を経過しながらたくさんの(八百万)の神々が生まれてこの国を統治していったとある。ここまでは世界中の多くの国や民族に伝承されている汎神論の世界観と同じである。そこに4世紀までには道教が伝わり、6世紀には仏教が伝わってきた。これらが宮中の権力者の支持を得ながら習合し、体系づけられ、儀式や呪法などが作られていったと考えられる。

5. Gods and the Buddha

A country where the gods and the Buddha have always coexisted

It is said that Japanese people are not particularly religious. It's true that we take newborn babies to a Shinto shrine to be blessed, hold Christian weddings, and Buddhist funerals. At New Year we pray to our *kamidana* (Shinto home shrine) and at *Obon* to our *butsudan* (Buddhist home altar), and we buy sweets for Valentine's and Christmas. It's not that we don't believe in religion at all, but rather that we pick-and-mix the way we use them.

Even in the precincts of a shrine or temple there may be an *inari* fox deity or a *tenjinsama* god, which many foreigners who have grown up under a strict monotheistic religion find hard to understand.

□厳格な strict
□弔う mourn for
□敷地 precinct
□稲荷 fox deity
□一神教 monotheistic religion
□外国人 foreigner

The ancient land of the gods

The creation myths of Japan (except for the Ainu and Ryukyu) as told in the *Kojiki* (Record of Ancient Matters) and *Nihonshoki* (Chronicles of Japan), relate how Izanagi and Izanami, the god-couple descended from the gods in heaven, gave birth to the Japanese islands, and their descendants. Amaterasu and Susano-o over time birthed "countless" gods who ruled over the country. This is a similar pantheistic worldview as in many countries and nations around the world. Then, however, Taoism was introduced around the fourth century, and Buddhism in the sixth century. With the support of influential people at court, these practices were then syncretized and systematized with rituals and incantations.

□伝説 myth
□末裔である descended from
□日本列島 Japanese islands
□子孫 descendants
□汎神論の世界観 pantheistic worldview
□道教 Taoism
□権力者 influential people
□習合する syncretize
□体系づける systematize
□呪法 incantation

神道と仏教の競合と混在の歴史

　なかでも仏教は大きな力を持つようになり、「日本の神々は、仏教の仏が仮の姿をとったもの」だとする説「本地垂迹説」が主流になった。アマテラスは「大日如来」の化身、応神天皇を祀る八幡様は「八幡大菩薩」（菩薩は仏をめざす修行者）といった具合で、神道支持勢力が取り込まれた。これがもう一度大きく変わるのは明治維新である。

　維新の旗印は、アマテラスから神武天皇につながる血脈を誇る天皇による親政が再開された「王政復古」にある。神政一致だ。外来の仏教は廃すべきとなり、寺院や仏像を破棄する「廃仏毀釈」運動も起きた。仏教軽視、神道復活の流れは太平洋戦争終了まで続いた。戦後は天皇の人間宣言と占領軍の神道指令、政教分離政策で、国家神道は終わりとなる。

History of the rivalry and coexistence of Shinto and Buddhism

Buddhism particularly became very powerful, and the theory that Shinto gods are the earthly manifestations of the heavenly buddhas and bodhissatvas became mainstream. Amaterasu became Dainichi Nyorai, while Hachiman, as who Emperor Ōjin was deified, was assimilated as Hachiman Great Bodhissatva (a bodhissatva is a trainee Buddha).

This underwent another big change in the Meiji Restoration, the objective of which was to restore to power the imperial line that boasted an unbroken connection to Emperor Jinmu, who was descended from Amaterasu. This was effectively a theocracy. Buddhism was seen as a foreign import and should be abolished, and there was the *haibutsu kishaku* movement to destroy Buddhist temples and statues. The drive to banish Buddhism and revive Shinto continued until the end of the Pacific War. Shinto ceased to be the state religion with the emperor's public renunciation of divinity and the occupation's Shinto Directive designed to effect the separation of state and religion.

□仮の姿 earthly manifestation

□説 theory

□主流 mainstream

□修行者 trainee

□明治維新 Meiji Restoration

□旗印 objective

□神政一致 theocracy

□廃す abolish

□太平洋戦争 Pacific War

□天皇の人間宣言 emperor's public renunciation of divinity

□政教分離 separation of state and religion

神社では手を打ち、寺では手を合わせる

　神仏を**使い分ける**日本人の習慣は、神社と寺での祈り方の違いに出る。まず神社での**作法**。鳥居をくぐると参道の脇に「**手水**」場がある。ここで口と手を清めたら、神殿の前に立ち、梁にかかった大きな鈴から垂れる綱を揺すって神様を呼ぶ。姿勢を正して小銭の「**賽銭**」を入れたら「二礼二拍手一礼」を行う。2度お辞儀をし、2度手を打ちならし、最後にもう一度お辞儀をするのである（神社によって回数が違ったりする）。この拍手を「かしわ手」という。なお、葬礼など**凶事**の際は、手を打っても音を出さないようにするとの決まりもある。一方、寺での祈りは静かに両手を合わせるだけで、感謝の気持ちを表している。

左：手水で穢れを落とす
右：鈴を鳴らして神を呼び起こす

L: Washing Hands to Cleanse Ritual Impurities,
R: Ringing a Bell to Call Out the Deity

Clap your hands at shrines, and bring your hands together at temples

The custom of Japanese people to differentiate the way of practising Shinto and Buddhism can also be seen in the different ways of praying at shrines and temples. First, the etiquette at shrines. As you pass through the *torii*, you will see a water trough to one side where you can cleanse your hands. Then, standing before the shrine, shake the rope hanging from the large bell hanging from a beam to summon the *kami*. Stand up straight and throw some change into the offertory box, then perform the bowing and clapping ritual: bow twice, clap your hands twice, then bow once more (the sequence may vary according to the shrine). This type of clapping is called *kashiwade*. At a funeral, or after an accident or disaster, you should not make any sound as you clap. On the other hand, when praying at a temple you simply bring your hands together in silence to express your thanks.

ちょうず ば
手水場
A water trough

□ 使い分ける differentiate
□ 作法 etiquette
□ 手水場 water trough
□ 梁 beam
□ 鈴 bell
□ 綱 rope
□ 賽銭 money offering
□ 二礼二拍手一礼 bow twice, clap your hands twice, then bow once more
□ 凶事 accident or disaster
□ 一方 on the other hand

6. 民間信仰

21

天神様、弁天様、お稲荷様

　神様なのか仏様なのか区別がつきにくい**聖地**がたくさんあるのも日本の特徴で、多くは庶民の**現世利益**を願う素朴な信仰対象である。たとえば「天神様」は、もともと天候を支配する神だったが、学者であり政治家でもあった菅原道真 (845–903) が**讒訴**によって九州に**左遷**された。その死後、**天変地異**が起こり、**要人**が変死するなどして「道真のたたり」と噂された。これに驚いた朝廷は彼を天神として**祀った**のが起源であり、**以後**、学問の神様、子供の神様として全国に広まり、今も受験生がお参りしている。また、「弁天様」こと「弁財天」は、お釈迦様を守る神のひとりだが、日本では**蓄財**と**技芸**とくに音楽の神様とされ、芸者さんや**水商売**に従事する人の信仰を集めている。「お稲荷様」は大昔の豪族である秦氏の家で祀られたものだが、稲つまり**豊穣**を叶える神様として広まり、それが**商売繁盛**の神になり、たくさんの小さな赤い鳥居と神の使いである白い狐を奉納する人が増えた。狐の好物として**油揚げ**を供えている光景も見かける。

6. Folk Beliefs

Tenjin, Benten, and Inari

It is often difficult to discern whether a sacred site in Japan is Buddhist or Shinto, and many are simply dedicated to a desire to gain material benefit through prayer. For example, Tenjin was originally a god that governed the weather. However, after the death in exile of the scholar and politican Sugawara no Michizane (845–903), who had been falsely accused and banished to Kyushu, many important personages there met a violent death in natural disasters rumored to be the result of Michizane's curse. The shocked court subsequently deified him as Tenjin, who thenceforth became known throughout the land as the god of scholarship and children, and even now students taking exams visit Tenjin shrines. Benten, also known as Benzaiten, is one of the deities that protects Shakyamuni, but in Japan she is also the goddess of wealth and of the arts, particularly music, so is worshiped by geisha and other workers in the nightlife business. Inari was worshipped long ago by the powerful Hata clan, and became known as the god of rice and bountiful harvests, and later as the god of good business, so more and more people made offerings of numerous small red *torii* and white fox messengers. Sometimes offerings of deep-fried tofu, which foxes are known to like, can also be seen.

□聖地　sacred site
□現世利益　material benefit
□讒訴　false accusation
□左遷する　banish
□天変地異　natural disaster
□要人　important personage
□たたり　curse
□祀る　deify
□以後　thenceforth
□学問　scholarship
□蓄財　wealth
□技芸　art
□水商売　nightlife business
□豊穣　bountiful harvest
□商売繁盛　good business
□油揚げ　deep-fried tofu

おめでたいのは「七福神」

　神様は1人よりたくさんの方がありがたい気持ちがするのは庶民の心。福をもたらす7人の神を集めたのが日本独特の「七福神」。メンバーは、「大黒天」「毘沙門天」「弁財天」「布袋」「福禄寿」「寿老人」「恵比寿」で豊作、長生き、金持ち、美人にという庶民的な願いを叶えてくれる神様たち。豊漁の神「恵比寿」以外は、ヒンドゥー教や道教などに起源をもつ多国籍軍団でもある。そしてこの七福神が、金銀やサンゴなどの宝物を満載して乗ってくるのが「宝船」で、元旦の夜にこの夢を見ると、夢が叶うといわれた。また、正月には、いろいろな場所に祀られているこれらの神様をお参りする「七福神めぐり」ツアーに出かける人も少なくない。

七福神と宝船
Seven Gods of Fortune and the Treasure Ship

The Seven Lucky Gods

Japanese people generally feel that lots of gods are luckier than one, and the *shichifukujin,* or seven lucky gods are unique to Japan. They include Daikokuten, Bishamonten, Benzaiten, Hotei, Fukurokuju, Jurōjin, and Ebisu, and grant the kind of wishes that appeal to ordinary people, such as bountiful harvests, long life, wealth, and beauty. Other than Ebisu, the god of fishermen, they are a multinational group originating in, amongst others, Hinduism and Taoism. And if these Seven Lucky Gods in their treasure ship laden with gold, silver, coral and other precious items, appear in your dreams on January 1, it is said your wishes will be granted. Also, at New Year quite a few people tour several locations where these gods are enshrined.

□日本独特 unique to Japan
□七福神 seven lucky gods
□豊作 bountiful harvest
□美人 beauty
□庶民 ordinary people
□以外 other than
□起源をもつ originating
□多国籍軍団 multinational group
□宝船 treasure ship
□叶う be granted
□祀られている be enshrined

ウソをつくと怖い「えんま様」

俗世間の願い事だけをきく神様ばかりではない。人気アニメ『ドラゴンボール』にも登場する「閻魔大王」は、**地獄の裁判官**であり、死者の生前の罪を裁いて罰を与えるおそろしい存在だ。その場のがれのウソをついても簡単に見破られてしまう。だから昔の子供たちは、「ウソをつくと、えんま様に舌を抜かれるぞ」と大人たちに脅かされたものである。**反面、**その強面の霊力を借りたいときもある。だからこの神様に祈るときは真剣だ。ちなみに好物はこんにゃくだとされる。

子供と地域の神様「お地蔵さん」

頭をそった小さな子供のような表情の「地蔵」は、日本中のいたるところに祀られている。**信仰上の位置づけは諸説**あるのだが、要するに地獄でも現世でも子供の姿でやってきてくれて疫病や**飢餓**などの苦難から救ってくれるのがこの神様。子供の健やかな成長を祈ったり、不幸にして早く死んだ子供の霊を慰めるために祀られることもある。京都などでは、お盆の時期に近所の地蔵堂の前に集まって祈り、大人たちからお菓子をふるまわれたりする「地蔵盆」という行事がある。

Lord Enma, the bane of liars!

Gods do not only listen to your mundane wishes. Enma Daio appears in the popular manga *Dragon Ball* as King Yemma, the fearsome judge of hell who punishes people according to the sins they committed when alive. He easily sees through anyone who lies in order to escape, and that's why in the past adults threatened children with, "If you lie, Lord Enma will pull out your tongue!" On the other hand, there are times when you want to borrow his miraculous power and so people also pray to him in earnest. Incidentally, his favorite food is said to be *konnyaku*, or devil's tongue jelly.

☐ 俗世間の願い事 mundane wish

☐ 地獄の裁判官 judge of hell

☐ 罪 sin

☐ 見破る see through

☐ 舌 tongue

☐ 反面 on the other hand

☐ ちなみに incidentally

☐ こんにゃく devil's tongue jelly

Jizō: god of children and travelers

Jizō, who really looks like a small child with a shaved head, is worshipped all over Japan. There are various theories about his religious status, but at the end of the day he is the deity who appears in child form in hell and on earth to save us from epidemics, starvation, and other sufferings. People also pray to him for the healthy growth of children, and to comfort the souls of children who had the misfortune of dying young. In Kyoto and some other places, there is a Jizō Festival during Obon when people gather before the local Jizō hall to pray, and the adults pass around sweets.

☐ 信仰上の位置づけ religious status

☐ 諸説 various theories

☐ 疫病 epidemic

☐ 飢餓 starvation

☐ 苦難 suffering

☐ 慰める confort

☐ ふるまう pass around

富士山信仰

　2013年6月、ユネスコは富士山を**世界文化遺産**として認定した。山なのに**自然遺産**でないのは、この山が古くから日本人の**信仰の対象**として神聖視され、また和歌や**浮世絵**などの題材ともなって、日本文化の重要な構成要素だったと認定したからだ。**山岳信仰**は古くから各地にあるが、富士山信仰が盛んになったのは江戸時代半ばからといわれる。富士をご神体とする浅間神社に詣でるために、庶民たちが仲間（講）を集める「富士講」が江戸と**周辺各地**に生まれ、頂上に上って日の出を仰ぐ「ご来光」がイベントのハイライトとみなされるようになった。

「おみくじ」は神様からのエール

　米国で中華料理店に行くと食後に、「おみくじ」の入ったクッキー（フォーチュン・クッキー）が出る。「占い」ごとが好きなのは洋の東西を問わない。日本では神社や寺院で「おみくじ」を売っている。おみくじにはいろんな種類があるが、一般的なのは「大吉」から「大凶」までを数段階に分けて表示し、それにしたがって**健康**や**恋愛**、**金運**、**勝負運**などの個別項目を占っているタイプだ。結果が良ければ喜ぶと同時に**有頂天**にならないようにと自戒し、悪ければ「次には好転する兆し」と**肯定的**に考えるべきだという。読み終わったおみくじは持ち帰らずに、境内に設けた専用の柵や樹木などに結びつける。神様との"縁"が結ばれた**という意味である**。ちなみにこのおみくじの70%は、山口県周南市にある女子道社という会社が作っている。

Fuji, the sacred mountain

In June 2013, UNESCO approved Mount Fuji as a World Heritage Site. The reason it is not considered a natural heritage despite being a mountain is that it has clearly been an important element in Japanese culture as an object of faith for Japanese people since ancient times, well-represented in art including *waka* poems and *ukiyoe* woodblock prints. Mountain worship has been practiced all over the country since antiquity, but Mount Fuji is said to have become a particular object of worship during the Edo period. Clubs were formed in Edo and the surrounding areas to visit Sengen Shrines worshipping Mount Fuji, with the climb to witness sunrise at the peak considered the highlight of the year.

□ 世界文化遺産 World Heritage Site
□ 自然遺産 natural heritage
□ 信仰の対象 object of faith
□ 浮世絵 *ukiyoe* woodblock print
□ 山岳信仰 mountain worship
□ 古くから since antiquity
□ 講 club
□ 周辺各地 surrounding areas
□ 日の出を仰ぐ witness sunrise

Omikuji: fortune telling by the gods

After dinner at a Chinese restaurant in the United States, diners are given a fortune cookie. People in the West and East both like fortune telling. In Japan, slips of paper telling your fortune, called *omikuji,* are sold at shrines and temples. There are various different types of *omikuji*, but the most common are those that grade fortunes from *daikichi* (excellent) to *daikyō* (terrible), with sections on health, love, finances, competitions, and so forth. If you get a good fortune, while being happy about it you should beware of being too elated, and if it's a bad fortune you should think positively that it's a sign that things will be better next time. After reading the fortune, you should tie it to the fence or tree provided rather than take it home with you. This signifies sealing your fate with the gods. Incidentally, 70% of these fortune slips are made by a company called Joshidōsha based in Shūnan City in Yamaguchi prefecture.

□ 占い fortune telling
□ 洋の東西 people in the West and East
□ 健康 health
□ 恋愛 love
□ 金運 luck with finance
□ 勝負運 luck in competition
□ 有頂天になる be too elated
□ 肯定的に positively
□ という意味である signify

おみくじ　*Omikuji*

4

つき合い
Social Events

1. お中元・お歳暮

22

モノに託して感謝の気持ちを伝える

シャイ（恥ずかしがり）な人が多い日本人は、愛情や感謝の心を言葉で伝えるのが苦手である。そのためかモノを贈呈することでその気持ちを伝えようとする。江戸時代には上司や得意先に贈る風習が定着し、この贈呈文化に目をつけた商売も盛んになり、それが今日の「お中元セール」「お歳暮セール」に繋がっている。

「お中元」は7月1日から15日までに贈る場合の呼び名で、それを過ぎて8月の立秋（7日前後）前までなら「暑中見舞い」、それ以降の月末までなら「残暑見舞い」となる。

一方、「お歳暮」は年末に交わす儀礼のことで、先祖の霊に捧げたものを新年の供え物にと、近所や実家、お世話になった人などに配るものだった。お歳暮の定番は塩鮭だったが、最近ではビールやハム、有名レストランのスイーツなどバラエティに富んでいる。

1. Mid-year and Year-end Gifts

Expressing your thanks with practical gifts

Many Japanese people are shy, and find it difficult to convey their feelings of affection and thanks through words. Maybe that's why we try to do so through giving gifts. The sale of *ochūgen* (mid-year) and *oseibo* (year-end) gifts derives from the custom of giving gifts to superiors and customers established in the Edo period, when businesses serving this custom thrived.

Ochūgen is the term used for gifts given between July 1 to 15, and those given in August around the beginning of autumn according to the old lunar calendar are called *shochū mimai*, or inquiries after one's health in midsummer. From then until the end of the month they are called *zansho mimai*, inquiries after one's health in the lingering summer heat.

Oseibo, on the other hand, refers to the etiquette for the year's end, when the offerings to the souls of ancestors were distributed as New Year gifts to family, neighbors, and people who helped you. A great variety of gifts are given today, from beer and ham to sweets from famous restaurants.

□恥ずかしがり shy
□愛情 affection
□言葉で through words
□伝える convey
□上司 superior
□得意先 customer
□風習 custom
□定着する establish
□立秋 the beginning of autumn
□暑中見舞い inquiries after one's health in midsummer
□残暑 lingering summer heat
□儀礼 etiquette
□先祖の霊 soul of ancestor
□塩鮭 salted salmon

2.上座・下座

23

主客・上下の人間関係で決まる座席

　商談で応接間に通される、車に乗る、料亭の座敷に座るといった際に、互いの人間関係を見て、誰がどこに座り自分がどこに座るべきかをひどく気にするのが日本人である。海外ならせいぜいレディーファーストのマナーがあるくらいだが、日本では主客の関係、役職・年齢の上下関係などを見て「上座・下座」を決めたり少しでも上位の席を譲り合ったりする習慣がある。

　日本風の座敷なら上座は「床の間」の近くになる。床の間というのは座敷の一部を少し高くし、そこに花や掛け軸を飾るようにしたもので、寺院において燭台や香炉などを置いたのが始まりだとされ、神聖な空間だった。そして入口に近い場所ほど下座になる。これがエレベーターの中だと操作ボタンのある奥側が上座で、操作ボタンの前が下座になり、タクシーでは後部座席で運転席の後ろが上座、運転席の隣が下座になる。電車などでは進行方向に向かって窓側が上座、後ろ向きの通路側が下座になる。その中間の場所にもそれなりのランクがある。ややこしいようだが、快適で万一の際の安全度が高いほど上座になり、快適でなくても何かの用事ですぐ出入りしてゲストや上司に貢献できそうな場所が下座という点では一貫性はある。

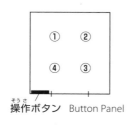

エレベーターの中 Inside an Elevator

日本料亭 At a Japanese Restaurant

タクシーの中 Inside a Taxi

2. Seating Etiquette

Seating arrangements for the host and guests decided by social hierarchy

When being shown into a drawing room, getting into a car, or sitting down for a meal at a traditional restaurant for business negotiations, Japanese people pay close attention to their social status in comparison with the other parties in order to decide where they should sit. Abroad you have at most the "ladies first" rule, but in Japan there is the custom for host and guest to consider their relative status in terms of relationship, position and age to decide whether to take one's place in a position of greater or lesser honor, and to offer even just a slightly better seat to each other.

In a Japanese style room, the place of highest honor is that closest to the *tokonoma* alcove. The *tokonoma* is slightly raised above the level of the floor, and decorated with flowers and a hanging scroll or other ornament. It is said to originate in the sacred space in temples where a candlestick or incense burner was placed. The place of least honor was by the door. In an elevator, the place of honor is furthest inside, while the spot by the button panel is the spot of least honor; in taxis the seat behind the driver is the place of honor, and least honor beside the driver; and in trains the window seat facing the direction of travel is the place of honor, with your back to the direction of travel is least honor. Even within these general outlines, the positions are ranked. It seems terribly complicated, but generally the seats of honor are in the most comfortable and safest seats in an emergency, while the least comfortable and most convenient seats to come and go in the service of your superiors are the positions of least honor.

□商談 business negotiation
□応接間 drawing room
□料亭 traditional restaurant
□ひどく気にする pay close attention to
□主客 host and guest
□役職 position
□上座・下座 position of greater or lesser honor
□掛け軸 hanging scroll
□燭台 candlestick
□香炉 incense burner
□神聖な空間 sacred space
□奥側 furthest inside
□隣 beside
□進行方向に向かって facing the direction of travel
□窓側 window seat
□ややこしいようだが It seems terribly complicated
□快適で comfortable
□万一の際 in an emergency

3. 宴会

24

進行役である「幹事」の大切な役目

結婚式の披露宴に代表される**祝い事**や大事な商談相手の**接待**などのために催されるパーティーが「宴会」である。日本の伝統的な宴会で重要な役目を果たすのが「幹事」である。幹事は、**会場**や**料理の手配**、**参加者**への連絡、送迎の手配、**宴の演出**さらには**会計**までのすべてを、ホストに**代わっ**て取り仕切る。

幹事は、宴の進行順序や**賓客**たちの序列を把握していなくてはならない。**乾杯**をするにしても、誰にその「音頭」をお願いすべきか、どういった「余興」が用意されているかも考えておかねばならない。ことに披露宴のようなめでたい席では、言葉の使い方にも気をつかい「終わる」を「お開きにする」などと言い換えられなくてはならない。

「手締め」でクロージング

日本的な宴会のクロージングでは**独特**の「**手締め**」(または「**手打ち**」)が行われる。ものごとが**無事**に終了したことを祝って、**掛け声とともに手拍子**を打つ。「**手締め**」にもいくつかのパターンがある。誰かが「**お手を拝借**」と声をかけたのを**合図**に、「ヨォー」と応じ、「3・3・3・1」のリズムを3回繰り返して手を打つのが「3本締め」。1回だけなのが「1本締め」。シンプルに「ヨォー、バン」と手を打つのは「1丁締め」という。だが日本人でも、この「1丁締め」を「1本締め」と**間違う**人が少なくない。

3. *Enkai*: Parties

The important role of *kanji* (organizer)

The parties held on celebratory occasions, such as a wedding reception, or to entertain a business client are called *enkai*. In a traditional Japanese *enkai*, the *kanji* plays an important role, dealing with everything on behalf of the host, from arranging the venue and the catering, contacting the participants, and seeing to the welcome and send-off, to directing the proceedings and settling the bill.

　　The *kanji* must have a firm grasp of the order of proceedings and the rank of the guests. He must also consider who to ask to propose the toast, and what kind of entertainment to offer. In the case of a felicitous occasion such as a wedding reception, he should also consider what words to use, such as using *ohiraki ni suru* instead of the word *owaru* (finish) to signal the end of the party.

☐結婚式の披露宴 wedding reception
☐祝い事 celebratory occasion
☐接待 entertain a business client
☐会場 venue
☐料理 catering
☐参加者 participant
☐宴の演出 directing the proceeding
☐会計 settling the bill
☐代わって on behalf of
☐賓客 guest
☐序列 rank
☐乾杯 toast
☐余興 entertainment
☐めでたい felicitous

Tejime at the end of the party

A traditional Japanese closing for a party is the characteristic *tejime,* or ceremonial handclapping (also known as *teuchi*) and accompanying shouts, which is carried out to indicate thanks for the successful conclusion of proceedings. There are various different patterns for the clapping. The *sanbon-jime* is the one where, upon the cue of "*Yō!*" participants clap a rhythm of 3–3–3–1 three times. The same rhythm carried out only once is called *ippon-jime*. The *itchō-jime* variation is a single clap upon the cue of "*Yō.*" However, even some Japanese people confuse the *itchō-jime* for *ippon-jime*.

☐独特の characteristic
☐手締め ceremonial handclapping
☐掛け声とともに accompanying shout
☐合図 cue
☐間違う confuse

気を許せない「無礼講」

　職場の仲間で催す宴会では上司も部下も出席するが、部下が遠慮しては宴を楽しめないだろうとの配慮から、上司が「今日の宴は『無礼講』でやろう」と声をかける。意味は「上下の礼儀を無視した仲間」ということだ。だが、だからといって羽目をはずし過ぎてはならない。「くつろいで良い」というニュアンスであって、「失礼な言動も大歓迎」というわけではない。ま、どんな宴席でも共通の心得ではあるが……。

Bureikō: laying aside formality

Bosses and general employees all attend workplace parties, but out of consideration for subordinates feeling too constrained to enjoy the party, the boss may announce "Today's party is *bureikō*," which indicates that the normal formalities between subordinates and their superiors need not be adhered to. However, you should not overdo it. It has the nuance of, "It's okay to relax," but that's not to say that rude behavior will be welcomed. Well, it's the same at any kind of party...

☐ 職場 workplace

☐ 部下 subordinate

☐ 配慮 consideration

☐ 羽目をはずし過ぎる overdo

☐ くつろいで良い It's okay to relax.

☐ 失礼な言動 rude behavior

4.あいさつ

25

「おじぎ」の使い分けに出る秩序意識

　貴人に挨拶するのに、頭を下げ腰を曲げておじぎするのは日本人だけの風習ではないのだが、外国人の目にはとても「日本人的」に映るようだ。たしかに日本人は誰に対してもよくおじぎをする。握手するひとは少数だ。それに、マナー本に、「おじぎの角度を使いわけるように」と書かれているのも日本ならではだ。

　つまり相手に対する最上級のおじぎは上体を45度の角度にする。初対面の挨拶程度なら30度。知人や同僚との軽い挨拶なら15度などと書かれている。相手と自分との関係を秩序意識で考え、細かく形式化する礼儀作法の文化がまだ残っている。

　身近なところで最上級のおじぎを受けたければデパートやホテルの入り口などで従業員がしてくれる。

4. *Aisatsu*: Greeting People

Deciding the angle of a bow

Greeting a person of high rank with lowered head and back bent in a bow is not limited to the Japanese, but *ojigi* (bowing) seems to foreigners to be a very Japanese custom. It's true that Japanese people bow a lot, and few people shake hands. Japanese books on etiquette even include a guide to the angle of the bow for different occasions.

The angle of the most formal bow is 45°. For a first meeting, it is 30°, while a general greeting to acquaintances and colleagues is 15°. There is still a culture of precisely formulating your bow according to your status in relation to the other person.

If you want to experience the most formal bow at close quarters, the staff at the entrance to a hotel or department store will oblige.

□貴人 person of high rank

□おじぎ bow

□風習 custom

□握手する shake hands

□角度 angle

□最上級の the most formal

□初対面の first meeting

□知人 acquaintance

□同僚 colleague

□相手と自分との関係 your status in relation to the other person

□形式化する formulate

□身近なところで at close quarters

□従業員 staff

敬語も使いわける？

　身振りだけでなく敬語にもいろんな種類がある。これまでその種類は「尊敬語、謙譲語、丁寧語」の3つといわれてきたが、2007年に文化審議会国語分科会はもっと**細分化**して5種類だとの答申をまとめた。尊敬語は相手の動作やものを**高めて**いうものだが、謙譲語つまり自分や**話題**の対象を一段低くいうものには、**話題の中の相手方を高めている**場合と、話を聞いている**相手**を**高めている**場合に分けられるという。そして**丁寧な気持ちを表す言葉**にしても、話し手の気持ちを表す場合とものごとを示す言葉の先頭に「お」や「ご」をつけて**美化した言い方**をする場合があるとしている。ま、**たしかにそうなのだが**、**正直なところ**日本人でも**状況に応じて**常に**完璧な**敬語を使いこなすのは**難しい**。

Keigo: using polite language

Not only are there different gestures, but there are varying degrees of polite language too, called *keigo*. It had always been said there were three types, *sonkeigo* (honorific forms), *kenjōgo* (humble forms), and *teineigo* (polite forms), but in 2007 the National Language Subcommittee of the Council for Cultural Affairs announced that these would be further subdivided into five forms. *Sonkeigo* uses words to elevate the other person in speech, while *kenjōgo*, which places the speaker or topic of speech at a level below the other person, is divided into cases where the object of the topic is elevated and where the listener is elevated. And with regards to words that express politeness, there are cases where they express the speaker's feelings, and cases where honorific prefixes such as *o* and *go* are added to words to make the speech sound nicer. Well, that's all very well, but the truth is that even Japanese people find it difficult to use the correct *keigo* for the situation.

- □ 身振り gesture
- □ 敬語 polite language
- □ 尊敬語 honorific forms
- □ 謙譲語 humble forms
- □ 丁寧語 polite forms
- □ 細分化する subdivide
- □ 高める elevate
- □ 話題 topic of speech
- □ 話題の相手方 object of the topic
- □ 丁寧な気持ちを表す express politeness
- □ 美化した言い方をする make the speech sound nicer
- □ たしかにそうなのだが that's all very well
- □ 正直なところ the truth is that
- □ 状況に応じて for the situation

5

衣・食・住
Clothes, Food, and Homes

1. 着物・小物

26

「振袖」は未婚女性が着る

衣類を意味する普通の言葉「着物」は、時として**伝統的な**日本の衣装つまり「**和服**」、とくに女性たちの「**お召し物**」だけを意味する。なかでも**あでやか**さで**人目をひく**のは「振袖」である。その「和服」や「振袖」にもちょっとした**しきたり**がある。まず襟合わせだが、男女とも（**相手から見て**）左 手側の襟を外側に出して着ることはない。女性の洋服の場合と逆である。これは「左前」といって死者の着付け方であり、**運気が傾く**不吉なものとされる。また、**袖の長い**「振袖」は20歳前後の**未婚女性**が着る。既婚者や年齢を重ねた場合は袖の短い、図柄も比較的**地味な**「留袖」を着る。

男性の和服といえば「羽織」と「袴」だろう。「羽織」は**防寒**あるいは礼装用に着物の上から着て、**帯**で結ばない。袴はサイド・スリットが大きなズボンである。明治以降、女性でも学校の**卒 業 式**などでは袴を着けるようになった。

着物の間違った着方
（左前合わせ）

Kimono Dressing Error
(When Left Side is Next to the Skin)

1. Kimonos and Accessories

The *furisode* worn by unmarried women

The word "kimono" ordinarily means clothing, but it is sometimes used to mean traditional Japanese wear, that is, the word kimono as used in English, especially to refer to women's wear. This includes the eye-catchingly glamorous *furisode*. There are certain conventions in kimonos and *furisode*. First of all, for both men and women, the left flap of the kimono neckline (as seen by someone facing you) should never be on the outside. This is the opposite of Western-style women's wear. It is called *hidari-mae*, and it is the way used for dressing the dead, so is seen as bringing bad luck. The long-sleeved *furisode* is worn by unmarried women around the age of twenty, while married and older women wear the *tomesode*, which has shorter sleeves and a relatively subdued pattern.

Japanese wear for men include the *haori* and *hakama*. The *haori* is a short coat worn over the rest of the outfit to protect against the cold or for formal occasions, and is not secured with a sash. *Hakama* are wide, skirt-like trousers with side slits near the waist. Since the Meiji period, women have also worn *hakama* for school graduation ceremonies and other occasions.

□衣類 clothing

□伝統的な traditional

□和服 kimono

□お召し物 wear

□あでやかな glamorous

□人目をひく eye-catchingly

□しきたり convention

□相手から見て as seen by someone facing you

□運気が傾く bring bad luck

□袖の長い long-sleeved

□未婚女性 unmarried woman

□地味な subdued

□防寒 protect against the cold

□帯 sash

□卒業式 graduation ceremony

振り袖（左）と留袖（右）
Long-sleeved Kimono (*Furisode*, L) and
Short-sleeved Kimono (*Tomesode*, R)

117

礼服には「家紋」をつける

　結婚式や葬儀など改まった場所に着ていく**礼装**として、男性は羽織に女性は黒地の「留袖」などに、その家の「**家紋**」がついたものを着る。これを「紋付き」というが、背中、胸元、袖など紋をつける数(1・3・5)が増えるほど**格式**が高い。

　だが着物を着る日本人は**残念ながら**減っている。「あらたまった場で着るもの」とか「高級なものを身に付けるべき」といったイメージが定着したからだ。もっとカジュアルで、身近に接する機会としては、**旅館**で寝巻きとして出されたり、夏の衣料して用いられる「浴衣」だろう。もとは入浴時の着物だった。

The family crest imprinted on formal wear

Formal wear for occasions such as weddings and funerals, usually a *haori* for men and a plain black *tomesode* for women, is imprinted with the family crest, called a *kamon*. This can be on the back, sleeves, or chest, and the greater the number (1, 3, or 5) imprinted indicates a higher social status.

Unfortunately, however, fewer people are wearing kimono these days, and they have the image of being something only worn on formal occasions, or something for high-class people to wear. A more casual, everyday version might be the light cotton *yukata*, which is an item of summer clothing, and is provided by Japanese inns for sleeping in. Originally it was worn when visiting a bathhouse.

□礼装 formal wear
□家紋 family crest
□格式 social status
□残念ながら unfortunately
□旅館 Japanese inn
□もとは originally

正式な礼装
Formal Wear

着物に欠かせぬ小物類

　着物に欠かせぬものといえば、女性の場合には「帯」がある。華麗な図柄や変わった織り方をした幅の広い帯が普及し、10を超える結び方が生み出されるようになるのは江戸時代の半ばから。それまでは10センチ幅程度で、締める位置ももっと腰に近かった。

　男性の場合、昔なら脇差（小刀）を腰にさすことで威厳をもてたが、帯刀禁止の現代では、手に持つ「扇子」程度しかない。女性はこれを帯の胸元にさしたりする。ちなみに小さく折りたためる「扇子」の仕組みは、日本人が発明したものだといわれている。

　他にも着物に似合う小物としては、用途万能の木綿タオル「手ぬぐい」。身の回りの小物を入れる小さな袋で口元を紐で締める「巾着」、「のし袋」や懐紙などを入れるハンカチのような「袱紗」、女性が胸元に挟む小さな「匂い袋」などがある。

Essential accessories for kimono

One essential accessory that women cannot do without when wearing a kimono is the *obi*, or sash. Since the mid-Edo period, the most popular has been a wide *obi* with a sumptuous design or unusual weave, with over ten ways to tie it. Before then, the *obi* had only been about 10 cm wide and worn closer to the hips.

Long ago wearing a short sword stuck through the *obi* at the hip conferred an air of dignity on men, but after it was forbidden to do this they had to make do with a folding fan instead. Women also keep their fan in their *obi* near the breast. Incidentally, the small folding fan is apparently a Japanese invention.

Another small accessory that goes with a kimono is the *tenugui*, a multipurpose cotton towel. Others include the *kinchaku,* a small drawstring bag for keeping personal items in, the *noshibukuro* gift envelope, the *fukusa* silk cloth used for keeping things like tissue paper in, and the small scented sachet that women keep at their breast.

□帯 sash

□華麗な図柄 sumptuous design

□変わった unusual

□織り weave

□結び方 way to tie

□それまでは before then

□脇差 short sword

□威厳 air of dignity

□禁止 forbidden

□扇子 folding fan

□胸元 near one's breast, at one's breast

□発明 invention

□用途万能の multipurpose

□木綿 cotton

□巾着 drawstring bag

□匂い袋 scented sachet

2. 食品

27

米に対する格別の想い

　食事を意味する普通の言葉として「ご飯」という。これは米など穀物を炊くか蒸すかした食品のこと。「飯」を「めし」とも読むのは「召すもの」（食するもの）に由来する。日本人にとって食事とは穀物を蒸すか炊くかしたものであり、穀物の中でも米には特別な愛着を持つ。江戸期まで米は通貨であり、給与でもあった。

　子供たちが茶碗に「ご飯」の粒を付けたまま食事を終えようとすると、昔の親たちは必ずこう注意した。「お米という字は、八十八と書く。これはお百姓さんが八十八もの手間をかけてお米を作るという意味だから、ひと粒でも無駄にしたらバチが当たる」と。その親たちには、「自分たちは三食とも白米は食べられなかった」との思いがあった。貧困や戦後の食料不足も影響しているが、そもそも庶民が白米を日常的に食べるという習慣がなかったのだ。農家でさえ雑穀やイモ類が多かった。

2. Food

Special affection for rice

The usual word for a meal is *gohan*. This refers to a meal made from a grain such as rice that has been boiled or steamed. The *han* (飯) in *gohan* can also be read *meshi*, which originates in the phrase *mesumono,* an old word for food. For Japanese people, a meal consists of boiled or steamed grain, and of all the grains rice has a special place in their affections. Until the Edo period rice was also used as a currency and to pay salaries.

In the old days, any children leaving grains of rice in their bowl uneaten would be scolded by their parents as a matter of course. The kanji for rice (米) is made up of the characters 8–10–8 (八十八), which is the number 88, and children were told that this meant the farmer took eighty-eight steps and efforts to make that rice, so it was wrong to waste even one grain. Those parents also had in mind that they themselves were unable to enjoy white rice for all three meals. This was partly due to poverty and food shortages after the war, but in any case people were not in the habit of eating white rice every day. Even in farming families, they often ate various other grains and tubers.

□穀物 grain
□炊く boil
□蒸す steam
□愛着 affection
□通貨 currency
□茶碗 bowl
□お百姓さん farmer
□〜もの手間をかける
　　take〜steps and efforts
□ひと粒 one grain
□白米 white rice
□貧困 poverty
□食料不足 food shortage
□雑穀 various othe grains
□イモ類 tuber

「ご飯」をめぐるマナーあれこれ

　愛着ひとかたならぬ「ご飯」については、当然いろいろなタブーやマナーが生まれる。茶碗に盛ったご飯に箸を立ててはならない(死者への供物のときだけ)。お膳に汁物や椀もののおかずがある場合は、まず汁物から順繰りにムラなく食べる(片付け食い、一丁食いはタブー)。正式な会席料理では、「おかわり」をする際には、茶碗にひとくち残す。茶碗の受け渡しにはお盆を使う(じかでは不衛生)……等々。

「すし屋」体験のステップアップ

　最近の子供は、職人が待ち受けるすし屋に行っても「お皿が回ってないね」と不思議がる。回転寿司が普及し、「すし屋」の世界標準になってしまうと以下の話は無用になる。しかし、「ちゃんとした店」で楽しみたい人のために心得として4つほど書いておこう。

①すしネタを食べる順序は「うす味」(白身など)から。味の濃いもの、酢締めの光りものは最後に。
②旬のもの、地物を尊重して。店が自慢したいネタである。
③出されたらすばやく。寿司はすぐに乾いて風味が落ちる。おっと、しょうゆの付けすぎも禁物。二つに食いちぎろうとせず一口で。
④店の "符丁" は使わない。「お愛想」(会計を)、「あがり」(お茶を)、「むらさき」(しょうゆ)、「がり」(しょうが)、「さび」(わさび)などは、本来、店側の符丁だった。客が使うのは野暮かつ下品である。以上。

Table manners

With such a great affection for rice, of course various taboos and manners have developed. You should never stick your chopsticks into a bowl of rice (this is only done as an offering to someone who has died). If there is soup or other small dishes as part of the meal, you should eat a little of each in turn starting with the soup (wolfing them down, or polishing off each dish in turn is taboo). When partaking of a formal *kaiseki* meal, if you want a second helping of rice you should leave a small amount in your bowl. The bowl should be placed on a tray when passing it to someone (for sanitary reasons). And so on.

A step up from the sushi restaurant experience

These days, children going to a sushi restaurant where the chef is on standby for orders are surprised not to see ready-made dishes circulating on a conveyor belt as in a *kaitenzushi* bar. These have become the standard and what I am about to explain is unnecessary for them. However, for those who want to enjoy a "real" sushi restaurant, let me just give four examples of things to watch out for.

1) You should start with the milder flavor ingredients (such as white fish), and save the stronger flavors and pickled items for last.
2) Respect seasonal and local produce. The shop will want to show it off.
3) Eat it as soon as it's placed before you. Sushi quickly dries out and loses flavor. Oh, and don't drench it in soy sauce. Don't bite it in half, but eat it in one mouthful.
4) Don't use the restaurant's jargon. *Oaiso* for the bill, *agari* for more tea, *murasaki* for soy sauce, *gari* for ginger, *sabi* for wasabi, and so on were all originally jargon used by the staff, and sound uncouth and vulgar when used by a customer. I'll leave it at that.

□愛着 great affection
□ひとかたならぬ so much
□茶碗 bowl
□箸 chopsticks
□供物 offering
□汁物 soup
□順繰りに in turn
□ムラなく食べる eat a little of each
□片付け食い、一丁食い polishing off each dish in turn
□おかわり second helping
□お盆 tray
□じかで directly

□待ち受ける on standby for
□標準 standard
□無用 unnecessary
□ちゃんとした real
□心得 thing to watch out for
□うす味 milder flavor
□酢締め pickled
□旬 seasonal
□地物 local produce
□尊重する respect
□自慢する show off
□風味 flavor
□一口で eat in one mouthful
□符丁 jargon
□しょうが ginger
□野暮 uncouth
□下品 vulgar
□以上 leave it at that

「初物」を食べると寿命が延びる？

　四季折々の山海の産物を楽しんできた日本人は、「旬」に敏感である。「旬」とは10日という意味なので、ものごとの盛り、食材の本当においしい期間はわずか10日ほどということになる。江戸時代の庶民は、その旬が始まってすぐ、初めて市場に出る食材を「初物」と呼び、これを食べると「寿命が75日延びる」と言い訳しながら、多少高い値段でも手に入れようとした。カツオ、米、茶、ソバ、たけのこ、ナス、酒などが人気だった。江戸時代には「初鰹」1尾に10万円以上の値がつく過熱ぶり。幕府が禁じてもとまらなかった。

　ところで、なぜ「75日」なのか？　根拠はない。「人の噂も75日」などともいう。

たけのこの煮物
simmered bamboo shoots

枡に入れた米
rice in a *masu*

Does eating *hatsumono* extend your life?

Japanese people have long enjoyed marine and land produce as it is harvested and are particularly sensitive to the idea of *shun* (season). *Shun* means literally "ten days," and food is said to be truly delicious and at its best for just ten days. In the Edo period, right at the beginning of the season the people would call the first time an item reached market *hatsumono* ("first crop"), and would buy it even for a high price on the justification that it would "extend your life by seventy-five days." Bonito, rice, tea, soba noodles, bamboo shoots, eggplants, sake and so forth were popular. In the Edo period, the first bonito of the season could fetch a ridiculously high price of at least 100,000 yen for a single fish. Even when the government banned the practice, it didn't stop. But why seventy-five days? There doesn't seem to be any reason for this, although it is also said that, "Rumors persist for seventy-five days."

□山海の産物 marine and land produce
□敏感 sensitive
□初物 first crop
□寿命 life
□延びる extend
□〜と言い訳して on the justification that
□カツオ bonito
□たけのこ bamboo shoot
□ナス eggplant
□など and so forth
□禁ずる ban
□根拠 reason
□噂 rumor

28

3. 家

畳に座り、障子で仕切る暮らし方

　世界中の民族がそれぞれに**個性的な家**を作ってきた。手近な材料で作れて、できるだけ頑丈で、できるだけ**快適な家**をめざして。それは暮らし方の反映でもあった。**竪穴式住居**から始まった日本人の家は、14世紀頃には禅僧の書斎に模したという「書院造り」が生まれ、続く15世紀には趣味的な茶室の雰囲気を取り入れた「数奇屋造り」も生まれた。当初は有力な武士や高僧の**住まい**だったものが時代とともに庶民の間にも普及した。

　「日本的な住宅」に明確な**定義**はないが、畳を敷き詰め、襖や障子で部屋を**仕切り**、壁の一部に「床の間」をしつらえ、**庭に面して縁側を置く**ような空間をイメージする人が多いだろう。机やベッドを置かず、部屋の広さは変えられるようになっている。

障子のある和室
Japanese-style room with *shōji* sliding doors

3. Homes

Tatami rooms partitioned by *shoji*

All around the world people have distinctive ways of building their homes, striving to make the most comfortable and strongest home they can with the materials available to them, which also determine their lifestyle. The oldest known houses in Japan were the pit dwellings, while in the fourteenth century the *shoin zukuri* style modeled on the study spaces of zen monks came in, and in the fifteenth century the *sukiya zukuri* followed the aesthetics of the tea-ceremony room. Residences that initially were only available to powerful samurai or high-ranking priests over time became popular with ordinary people.

There is no clear definition of a Japanese style home, but most people probably have an image of *tatami* floors, rooms partitioned by *shōji* and *fusuma* sliding doors, a *tokonoma* alcove set into the wall, and a veranda facing onto the garden. Without fixed furniture like a desk or bed, the room sizes are flexible.

□ 個性的な distinctive
□ 材料 material
□ 快適な comfortable
□ 竪穴式住居 pit dwelling
□ 禅僧 zen monk
□ 茶室 tea-ceremony room
□ 住まい residence
□ 庶民 ordinary people
□ 定義 definition
□ 仕切る partition
□ 庭に面して facing onto the garden
□ 縁側 veranda

町家と長屋と農家

　周囲から独立した一戸建ての家に住むのが武士階級だとすれば、他の階級の人たちはどんな家に住んだのか？

　商人や職人たちが繁華街に集まり軒を並べて作った家が町家だ。間口の広さに応じて税金がかかることもあったので、奥に深く土間で繋がる「うなぎの寝床」という構造になった。賑やかな表通りの裏道には、少し貧しい人たちの長屋があった。流しと押入れと二間の部屋。井戸とトイレは共用で、全体の管理は持ち主に委託された「大家さん」の役目だった。屋根は樹皮を薄く剥いだものを敷いて石を載せていたが、後に瓦が多くなる。都会では自宅に風呂を持つ家は少数派で、公衆浴場「銭湯」を利用した。

　農家はいろんな機能を持ったスペースが必要になる。作業場や農具置き場、それに地域によっては牛馬など家畜の寝床も家の中に組み入れられた。たいていの農家には家の中心に煮炊きや暖房のために「囲炉裏」が作られていた。こちらの屋根は茅葺だ。

囲炉裏
Irori (Hearth)

Machiya, nagaya, **and** *nōka*

If detached residences were for the samurai class, what kind of houses did the other classes live in?

The merchants and the artisans were crowded into busy shopping streets, building houses called *machiya* side-by-side. Since the amount of tax was calculated by the width of the façade, the *machiya* stretched back in a long and narrow structure dubbed an "eel bed." In the backstreets behind the lively main street were the *nagaya* (long houses) of the less well-off. They consisted of a washing area, a storage space, and two rooms. The well and toilets were shared, the management of which was entrusted by the owner to a landlord. The roof was made of thin strips of bark, and secured with stones placed on top, although later tiles became common. Houses in the city with their own bath were in the minority, and people used public baths called *sentō*.

Nōka, or farmhouses, required certain spaces with specific functions including a work space and somewhere to store farm tools, and in some areas farm animals such as cows and horses had their sleeping quarters inside the house. At the center of nearly all farmhouses was the sunken hearth used for cooking and heating. These houses had thatched roofs.

□一戸建て detached residence
□階級 class
□商人 merchant
□職人 artisan
□繁華街 busy shopping street
□並べて side-by-side
□間口の広さ width of the façade
□うなぎの寝床 eel bed
□表通り main street
□裏道 backstreet
□貧しい人 the less well-off
□井戸 well
□共用 shared
□〜に委託された be entrusted by
□大家 landlord
□樹皮 bark
□瓦 tile
□公衆浴場 public bath
□農家 farmhouse
□家畜 farm animal
□寝床 sleeping quarter
□煮炊き cooking
□囲炉裏 sunken hearth
□茅葺 thatched

地鎮祭と風水

　家を建てたり大規模な土木工事を始める際に、今でも神事にもとづく「地鎮祭」が行われる。これは土地に住む神霊に許しをもらい、併せて工事も完成後も事故のないようにと願うためだ。「地鎮祭」は、土地の四隅に青竹を立て、**注連縄**を張り、**祭壇**を設けて行う。

　また家の**間取り**や配置については「**家相**」と呼んで、「**風水**」の考え方を取り入れることも多い。道教思想だから東アジア各地の風習と同じだ。これは**地形**や**方角**から吉凶を判断し、気の流れをよくする。たとえば玄関は東か東南がよく、台所や水回りの設備が北西にあると**家運が**傾き、悪い気が集まるところは魔力を持つ鏡や赤い色彩のものを置くのがよいといった具合だ。

地鎮祭

Shinto Ceremony to Consecrate
a Building Site

踏んではいけない畳の縁や敷居

　住む上でのしきたりもある。子供たちは、畳の縁や敷居を踏んではならないとしつけられる。理由は、それらが神聖な空間を守る境目「**結界**」と考えられたからという説がある。また**傷みやすい**部分だから大切にしたという説も**合理的**である。ついでにいえば座布団も踏んではならないものだった。お客が腰を据えるものだから失礼になる。

Purifying a building site

Even now, a *jichinsai* purification ceremony based on a Shinto ritual is carried out whenever starting construction on a house or large-scale building. This is to get permission from the god living on the land, and to pray that no accidents will occur either during construction or after completion. For the ceremony a piece of green bamboo is stood in each corner, a *shimenawa* sacred festoon is hung around the site, and an altar is set up.

Furthermore, elements of feng shui are often incorporated into the positioning and layout of the house, called *kasō*. This is a Taoist ideology that is practiced all over East Asia. The fortune of the land is judged according to its topography and bearings, and can be mitigated by adjusting the flow of energy. For example, a house with a front entrance facing east or south-east, with the kitchen and installations using water to the north-west, has a tendency to declining fortunes, so to counter this you can place a mirror, which is said to have magical powers, or a red object in spots where bad energy gathers.

□完成後 after completion
□注連縄 sacred festoon
□祭壇 altar
□間取り layout
□風水 feng shui
□思想 ideology
□地形 topography
□方角 bearing
□水回りの設備 installations using water
□家運が傾く tendency to declining fortunes
□悪い気 bad energy

Don't step on the border of the *tatami* or the doorsill!

There are certain conventions in Japanese houses. Children have it drummed into them not to step on the border of the *tatami* or the doorsill. One theory for this is that they traditionally mark the boundary of a sacred space, although another more practical theory holds that it was to protect a part that was easily damaged. Incidentally, you shouldn't stand on floor cushions either. Guests sit on them so it's rude to do so.

□しきたり convention
□縁 border
□敷居 doorsill
□しつける drum into
□境目、結界 boundary
□傷みやすい easily damaged
□合理的 practical
□座布団 floor cushion

4. 暮らし方

29

家長を中心に作られる秩序

　家は暮らし方の反映である。誰がどんな風に暮らすかで、空間や道具の生かされ方が決まる。日本では家長を中心に暮らし方の秩序が作られてきた。家長は父親あるいはその役を担う世帯主である。家長は上座に座り、食事も特別のお膳で一品多いし、風呂に入るのも一番先(湯を使い回すから)。一家が同じ食卓を囲んで団欒するような光景が生まれるのは20世紀(大正時代)になってからである。

正座とあぐら

　椅子がないのだから、畳か板の間に座るしかない。正座つまりあらたまった場合や僧侶や女性たちの座り方は、「屈膝座法」。脚を折り曲げ尻がかかとの上に来るように座る。一方、くつろいだ座り方は「あぐら」。尻をついて座るが脚を投げ出さず引き寄せる。「あぐら」は「胡座」と書く。イランやモンゴルなど中国西方の民族を「胡」と呼んだが、そこから伝わったとされる。正座は畳が普及するようになり、礼儀作法などが細かくなった後世のもので、むしろ「あぐら」や「立てひざ」「横座り」の方が普通だった。

4. Lifestyle

Life is ordered around the head of the family

The house reflects the lifestyle: who lives there and how determines how the space and contents are used. In Japan, the whole way of life is ordered around the head of the family, who is either the father or the householder fulfilling that role. He sits in the seat of highest honor, is served more elaborate meals, and is the first to take a bath (everyone takes turn using the same bathwater). It was only in the twentieth century (in the Taisho period) that the scene of a happy family sitting around the dinner table began to be seen.

□ 暮らし方 lifestyle
□ 反映 reflection
□ 家長 head of the family
□ その役を担う fulfilling that rule
□ 世帯主 householder
□ 風呂に入る take a bath
□ 団欒する sit in a circle happily
□ 光景 scene

Seiza and *agura*

Since there aren't any chairs, you have to sit on the *tatami* or wooden floor. *Seiza*, or kneeling with your bottom resting on your heels, is the way women and priests sit as well as the position used for formal situations. The informal sitting position is cross-legged—sitting with your bottom on the floor and your legs folded in front of you. This is called *agura* in Japanese, and is written 胡座, literally "barbarian sitting." The peoples of the countries to the west of China, such as Iran and Mongolia, were called "barbarians" and the term is thought to be derived from this. *Seiza* is part of the relatively new etiquette that developed after *tatami* became popular, whereas before that the norm was to sit cross-legged, *tatehiza* (sitting with one knee drawn up), or *yokozuwari* (sitting with your legs folded to one side).

□ 板の間 wooden floor
□ あらたまった場合 formal situation
□ 僧侶 priest
□ 〜から伝わる be derived from
□ 礼儀作法 etiquette

つましさと「もったいない」

　日本人の伝統的な暮らし方をひとことでいうなら「つましさ」だろう。質素倹約を心がけ、それを美徳とする社会だった。**無駄なものは買わず**、ものを大切にし、**壊れても修理するか転用して使い切る**。**着古した衣類**はもとより**糞尿**から**かまどの灰**まで役立つものであり、**専門の買取り業者**もいた。食べ物の調理法、保存方法も発達し、**漬物**や味噌・醤油などの**発酵食品**は日本食の基本でもある。

　こうしたつましい暮らしの中で人々の**口癖**になっていたのが「もったいない」だった。ルーツは**仏教用語**で、ものの本来のカタチ「**物体**」がなくなる**無常**さを嘆く言葉だったという。「MOTTAINAI」は、**大量生産・大量廃棄**の現代社会に反発する人たちの暮らし方を象徴する世界語でもある。

Frugality and *mottainai*

If I were to sum up the traditional Japanese lifestyle in one word, it would probably be "frugality." Society made a virtue out of simplicity and economy. People never bought unnecessary items and took care of those they had, repairing them when they broke or using them for different purposes to get the utmost out of them. Everything was recycled, from old clothes to ashes from the stove and human waste, and there were even specialist traders dealing in these. Methods of cooking and preserving food were also developed, with pickles and fermented foods like miso and soy sauce forming the basis of Japanese cuisine.

Within this frugal way of living, the word *mottainai* (What a waste!) came to be a stock phrase. It is rooted in Buddhist terminology lamenting the transience of things, with *mottai* referring to items in their original form, and *nai* to their non-existence. The word *mottainai* has now come to symbolize the lifestyle of those who are against the mass-consumerism prevalent in our current society.

□ ひとことでいう sum up
□ つましさ frugality
□ 質素倹約 simplicity and economy
□ 美徳 virtue
□ 無駄な unnecessary
□ 転用する use something for different purposes
□ 〜を使い切る get the utmost out of
□ 着古した衣類 old clothes
□ 糞尿 human waste
□ かまど stove
□ 業者 trader
□ 方法 method
□ 漬物 pickles
□ 発酵食品 fermented food
□ 口癖 stock phrase
□ 仏教用語 Buddhist terminology
□ 無常 transience
□ 嘆く lament
□ 大量生産・大量廃棄 mass-consumerism

6
その他
Miscellaneous

1. 年・月・時間

30

元号と西暦の両方を使う不便さ

　日本では「元号法」という法律があり、天皇が生きている間はひとつの元号(年号)を使うことが決められている。**昭和**、**平成**、**令和**というものだ。そして多くの**官庁**が**公文書**や**免許証**などを元号で記載している。法的には**強制**していないのだが……。

　一方、パスポートや**賞味期限**の表記などは**西暦**である。市販のカレンダーや新聞の**日付欄**などは元号と西暦を併記している。「平成19年は2007年」という具合に換算しなくてはならないから、日本人の多くは西暦と元号の年号をすぐには結びつけられない。

　古今東西、王や皇帝など**治世者**の**特権**は暦を決められることだった。**治世中**に**変事**があれば**縁起**をかついでめでたい言葉を選んで**改元**した。日本でもクーデターにより「大化」という元号が最初に生まれた(645年)。現在の「令和」は2019年5月1日にできた。

元号と西暦の対照表 Japanese to Western Calendar Converter

昭和 2 年	1927年	昭和13年	1938年	昭和24年	1949年	昭和35年	1960年	昭和46年	1971年
昭和 3 年	1928年	昭和14年	1939年	昭和25年	1950年	昭和36年	1961年	昭和47年	1972年
昭和 4 年	1929年	昭和15年	1940年	昭和26年	1951年	昭和37年	1962年	昭和48年	1973年
昭和 5 年	1930年	昭和16年	1941年	昭和27年	1952年	昭和38年	1963年	昭和49年	1974年
昭和 6 年	1931年	昭和17年	1942年	昭和28年	1953年	昭和39年	1964年	昭和50年	1975年
昭和 7 年	1932年	昭和18年	1943年	昭和29年	1954年	昭和40年	1965年	昭和51年	1976年
昭和 8 年	1933年	昭和19年	1944年	昭和30年	1955年	昭和41年	1966年	昭和52年	1977年
昭和 9 年	1934年	昭和20年	1945年	昭和31年	1956年	昭和42年	1967年	昭和53年	1978年
昭和10年	1935年	昭和21年	1946年	昭和32年	1957年	昭和43年	1968年	昭和54年	1979年
昭和11年	1936年	昭和22年	1947年	昭和33年	1958年	昭和44年	1969年	昭和55年	1980年
昭和12年	1937年	昭和23年	1948年	昭和34年	1959年	昭和45年	1970年	昭和56年	1981年

1. Dates and Times

The inconvenience of using both the Japanese and Western calendars

According to Japan's Era Name Law, the name of an era is used as long as an emperor is living. Showa, Heisei, and Reiwa are the era names that have been used from 1868 to the present. Many government offices use era names on official documents, licenses, and such like, even though it's not compulsory by law.

On the other hand, the Western calendar is used for things like passports and use-by dates. Both systems are used for calendars and newspaper datelines. Many Japanese people are not immediately able to convert between them, so both are shown, as in "Heisei 19, or 2007."

All over the world, it has historically been the privilege of rulers from kings to emperors to decide on calendar naming. If a disaster occurred during their rule, they would take it as an omen and choose an auspicious word for a change in era name. In Japan, too, a coup d'etat in the year 645 prompted the new era called Taika, literally "great change." The current Reiwa era started on May 1, 2019.

□元号 name of an era
□昭和 Showa era
□平成 Heisei era
□令和 Reiwa era
□官庁 government office
□公文書 official document
□免許証 license
□強制 compulsory
□賞味期限 use-by date
□西暦 Western calendar
□日付欄 dateline
□すぐには immediately
□古今東西 all over the world
□特権 privilege
□治世中に during one's rule
□変事 disaster
□縁起 omen
□改元 change in era name

昭和 57 年	1982年	平成 4 年	1992年	平成 15 年	2003年	平成 26 年	2014年
昭和 58 年	1983年	平成 5 年	1993年	平成 16 年	2004年	平成 27 年	2015年
昭和 59 年	1984年	平成 6 年	1994年	平成 17 年	2005年	平成 28 年	2016年
昭和 60 年	1985年	平成 7 年	1995年	平成 18 年	2006年	平成 29 年	2017年
昭和 61 年	1986年	平成 8 年	1996年	平成 19 年	2007年	平成 30 年	2018年
昭和 62 年	1987年	平成 9 年	1997年	平成 20 年	2008年	平成 31 年	2019年
昭和 63 年	1988年	平成 10 年	1998年	平成 21 年	2009年	令和 元 年	2019年
昭和 64 年	1989年	平成 11 年	1999年	平成 22 年	2010年	令和 2 年	2020年
平成 元 年	1989年	平成 12 年	2000年	平成 23 年	2011年	令和 3 年	2021年
平成 2 年	1990年	平成 13 年	2001年	平成 24 年	2012年	令和 4 年	2022年
平成 3 年	1991年	平成 14 年	2002年	平成 25 年	2013年	令和 5 年	2023年

2. 縁起かつぎ

31

穢れをはらう「塩」の霊力

　日本人のしきたりに共通している重要な概念の一つは「穢れと清め」である。不吉な気が取りつくのが「穢れ」であり、それを振り払う所作や儀式が「清め」になる。清めの儀式によく使われるのが「塩」である。葬儀に参列した後には「清めの塩」が配られ、服に振ったり靴で踏むなどする。相撲で力士が土俵に撒くのも、地鎮祭で塩を盛るのもこの「清め」である。

　混同されがちなのは、料亭など商売の家が玄関口に円錐形に盛る「盛り塩」だ。これは意味がまったく違う。由来は中国の故事で、秦の始皇帝が3000人もの愛妾宅を牛車で廻っていたのだが、ある愛人が、「牛は塩をなめたがる」と思いついて自宅の玄関先に盛り塩したら、始皇帝の牛車がしばしば立ち寄るようになったという。客を引き寄せるおまじないなのだ。

金と人を呼ぶ「招き猫」と「熊手」

　客商売で縁起が良いとされるものに「招き猫」と「熊手」もある。猫が右手(右前脚)をあげているのは金運を招き、左手は人を招くという。欲張って両手をあげて「バンザイ」すると倒産だというオチがつく。1990年頃から招き猫は世界中に広がった。ただし「ウェルカム」と招く際の手の動きが日本と逆で手の平が自分に向いている。

2. Attracting Luck

The miraculous power of salt to cleanse impurities

One important concept evident in all Japanese customs is that of *kegare* (impurity) and *kiyome* (purification). *Kegare* is when bad energy takes hold, and *kiyome* describes the processes and rituals to get rid of it. One thing that is often used in *kiyome* rituals is salt. After attending a funeral, purifying salt is brought out and scattered on people's clothes, and on the ground for them to walk on it with their shoes. Sumo wrestlers sprinkle salt in the ring to purify it, and forming piles of salt in the ceremony to purify a new building site also serves the same function.

It is easy to confuse this with the little conical heaps of salt in the entrances to traditional restaurants and other businesses, which have a very different meaning. This practice is said to be based on the story of the Chinese Qin emperor Shi Huang-ti, who would do the rounds of his 3,000 concubines in an ox cart, and one of his lovers had the foresight to place some salt beside her door for the oxen to lick so that they would come to her more often. It's a talisman to attract customers.

The "beckoning cat" and "bear's paw" to attract money and people

The *maneki-neko* (beckoning cat) and *kumade* (bear's paw, or lucky rake) are considered lucky for outlets in the service industry. The cat with its right front paw raised is inviting money, and with its left paw raised is inviting people. If it has both paws raised in a "banzai" salute, though, it will end in bankruptcy for the business. The *maneki-neko* has become popular around the world since about 1990. However, unlike in Japan, it shows its "welcome" invitation with the palm of the hand facing towards itself.

□ 概念 concept
□ 穢れ impurity
□ 清め purification
□ 不吉な気 bad energy
□ 取りつく take hold
□ 振り払う get rid of
□ 所作 process
□ 儀式 ritual
□ 配られる be brought out
□ 撒く sprinkle
□ 地鎮祭 ceremony to purify a new building site
□ 塩を盛る form piles of salt
□ 混同する confuse
□ 円錐形の conical
□ 愛妾 concubine
□ 牛車 ox cart
□ 引き寄せる attract

□ 客商売 service industry
□ 縁起が良い lucky
□ 招き猫 beckoning cat
□ 熊手 lucky rake
□ 前脚 front paw
□ 倒産 bankruptcy

　「熊手」はまだ国際的とはいえないが、めでたい飾り物をたくさんつけた「熊手」を求めて、毎年「酉の市」に出かける人が多い。人も金もこれでかき集めたいからだ。この「熊手」よりマイナーだが、関連する縁起ものに「ちり取り」もある。

縁起ものの熊手（左）とちり取り（右）

Items with Good *Engi*: *Kumade* (L) and Dustpan (R)

おめでたい動物と植物

　吉祥をもたらす動物もたくさんいる。「鶴は千年、亀は万年」もの長寿とされるし、「めでタイ」の鯛、「苦労がないから不苦労」のフクロウもいれば、「なくした金やモノが帰る」というカエルもいる。植物なら「松、竹、梅」だろう。これは中国の「歳寒三友」（論語）の話からだという説が一般的だが、厳しい環境（冬）でも凛として生きる人の生き方がテーマなのであって、別にめでたい意味はない。日本的に変形された。祝い事にと、この名で売る酒もある。

The *kumade* isn't known internationally yet, but there are many people who go each year to the November fairs held at shrines to purchase one of these decorative lucky rakes. This is because they are said to attract people and money. Another lucky item, although less so than the *kumade*, is the *chiritori* dustpan.

☐ 酉の市 November fairs held at shrines

☐ 縁起物 lucky item

☐ ちり取り dustpan

招き猫
beckoning cat

Lucky animals and plants

There are also many auspicious animals. According to one saying, "Cranes live a thousand years, turtles for ten thousand years," while the word for sea bream in Japanese is *tai*, which matches the latter part of the word *medetai*, meaning "lucky." The owl is connected with the saying "He without hardship is untroubled" since the word for owl (*fukurō*) is homophonous with the word for "untroubled," while frogs (*kaeru*) are homophonous with the word "return" in the phrase "Lost objects and money will return." Lucky plants include the trio of pine, bamboo, and plum. The usual theory is that this is from the Chinese tale "Three Friends of Winter" (from *The Analects of Confucious*), but this is on the subject of people thriving in the harsh environment of winter, and doesn't especially mean they are lucky, which is a Japanese-style transformation. For celebratory occasions, there is a brand of sake named after them too.

☐ 吉祥をもたらす auspicious

☐ 鶴 crane

☐ 亀 turtle

☐ 鯛 sea bream

☐ 苦労 hardship

☐ フクロウ owl

☐ カエル frog

☐ 松 pine

☐ 竹 bamboo

☐ 梅 plum

☐ 論語 The Analects of Confucious

☐ 厳しい環境 harsh environment

☐ 凛として生きる thrive

☐ 別に not especially

☐ 変形 transformation

　日本的変形というなら「ダルマ」がある。元は壁に向かって9年も座禅して悟りを開いた中国の達磨大師である。貯金箱や選挙の勝利祈願に使われる人形になった。ずんぐり丸くて底部を重くした「起き上がり」人形タイプが多いので、転んでも何度でも立ち上がる「七転び八起き」がめでたいのだという。だが「手も足も出ない」姿から、無力な資産ゼロ状態になることも「ダルマになる」という。ややこしい。

ダルマ
Daruma (Bodhidharma)

嫌われる数字は4と9

　クリスチャンは、キリストが死んだとされる13日にちなんで、「13」を不吉な数字という。映画「オーメン」で有名になったが、ヨハネ黙示録に出てくる「666」も魔獣の数字だ。日本では、単なる語呂合わせだけを根拠に「4(死)」「9(苦)」が嫌われる。逆に「8」は喜ばれる。漢字の「八」が「末広がり」(将来幸運)だというしゃれである。

Speaking of Japanese-style transformations, there is the *daruma*. This originates in the monk Bodhidharma who attained enlightenment in China after meditating before a wall for nine years. Now, however, it is a doll used as a piggy bank or to pray for victory in an election. Many are squat and round, weighted at the base so they always return to the upright position, and since they always rise after a fall are considered lucky. On the other hand, since they lack arms and legs, those who are powerless with zero assets are also described as a *daruma*. It's complicated.

□悟り enlightenment
□貯金箱 piggy bank
□選挙 election
□勝利祈願 pray for victory
□底部 base
□起き上がり always return to the upright position
□無力な powerless
□ややこしい It's complicated.

The unlucky numbers 4 and 9

Christians consider the number 13 to be unlucky since it is said to be the day Christ died, while according to the Book of Revelations of St. John the number 666 represents the Devil, as made famous by the film *The Omen*. In Japan there is the simple word play of the numbers 4, a homophone for the word for "death," and 9, a homophone for the word for "suffering." On the other hand, the number eight is lucky, since the kanji 八 resembles an unfolded fan spreading toward the end, which represents increasing prosperity over the years.

□不吉な unlucky
□ヨハネ黙示録 Book of Revelations of St. John
□語呂合わせ word play
□逆に on the other hand
□末広がり spreading toward the end
□将来幸運 increasing prosperity over the years

147

3. 図像(ずぞう)

32

「家紋(かもん)」は一族(いちぞく)を表(あらわ)すマーク

　日本(にほん)の戦国時代(せんごくじだい)を描(えが)いた映画(えいが)などでは、将兵(しょうへい)たちが家紋(かもん)をつけた旗(はた)を振(ふ)りかざして合戦(かっせん)する。家紋(かもん)は着物(きもの)についていたり、食器(しょっき)や提灯(ちょうちん)、墓石(ぼせき)、のれんなどにもついている。それぞれに由緒正(ゆいしょただ)しい家柄(いえがら)であることを示(しめ)す一族(ぞく)(ファミリー)のマークである。同(おな)じような紋(もん)でも丸(まる)く囲(かこ)んであるとか、その丸(まる)も2重(じゅう)であるとかで本家(ほんけ)と分家(ぶんけ)など支族(しぞく)の違(ちが)いを示(しめ)している。天皇家(てんのうけ)にも「十六花弁(じゅうろくかべん)の菊(きく)」があり、日本政府(にほんせいふ)も中央(ちゅうおう)に7つ、左右(さゆう)に5つの花房(はなぶさ)についた「五七(ごしち)の桐(きり)」を用(もち)いている(500円(えん)硬貨(こうか))。日本(にほん)のパスポートには表面(ひょうめん)に菊(きく)、写真(しゃしん)のページには「五三(ごさん)の桐(きり)」がついている。法務省(ほうむしょう)所管(しょかん)だからだ。

　ほかにも織田信長(おだのぶなが)の「五葉木瓜(いつつばもっこう)」、徳川家康(とくがわいえやす)の「三(み)つ葉葵(ばあおい)」、前田利家(まえだとしいえ)の「梅鉢(うめばち)」など武将(ぶしょう)たちの家紋(かもん)がよく知(し)られている。

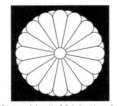

皇室(こうしつ)の紋(もん)「十六花弁(じゅうろくかべん)の菊(きく)」
Crest of the Imperial House of Japan
Sixteen-petaled Chrysanthemum

日本政府(にほんせいふ)の紋(もん)「五七(ごしち)の桐(きり)」
Crest of the Japanese Government
"5-7 Paulownia"

織田家(おだけ)の紋(もん)「五葉木瓜(いつつばもっこう)」
Crest of the Oda
5-Leaf *Mokkō*

徳川家(とくがわけ)の家紋(かもん)「三(み)つ葉葵(ばあおい)」
Crest of the Tokugawa
3-Leaf Hollyhock

前田家(まえだけ)の家紋(かもん)「梅鉢(うめばち)」
Crest of the Maeda
"*Umebachi*-style" plum blossom

3. Iconography

The *kamon* representing the clan

In films about Japan's Warring States period, you can see warriors going into battle brandishing a banner featuring the clan's *kamon*, or crest. This crest is also emblazoned on kimono, tableware oducts and lanterns, gravestones, *noren* curtains, and so on. It is the mark that shows the correct lineage and social standing of the family. A *kamon* that has one or more rings around it shows the different branches that were established separately from the main family. The imperial family's crest features the "sixteen-petalled chrysanthemum," while that of the Japanese government is the "five-seven paulownia" crest with seven blossoms on the center leaf and five on each side leaf (as on the 500 yen coin). On the front of the Japanese passport is the chrysanthemum, and on the photograph page is a five-three paulownia as used by the Ministry of Justice.

Apart from these, the crests of famous warlords are well-known, such as Oda Nobunaga's *itsutsuba mokkō* (which resembles a five-petaled flower), Tokugawa Ieyasu's *mitsuba aoi* (three hollyhock leaves), and Maeda Toshiie's *umebachi* (Japanese plum blossom).

□ 戦国時代 Warring States period
□ 将兵 warrior
□ 家紋 crest
□ 旗 banner
□ 振りかざす brandish
□ ～についている be emblazoned on
□ 食器 tableware
□ 提灯 lantern
□ 墓石 gravestone
□ 由緒正しい correct lineage and social standing
□ 本家 main family
□ 分家 branch
□ 天皇家 imperial family
□ 菊 chrysanthemum
□ 花房 blossom
□ 桐 paulownia
□ 硬貨 coin
□ 法務省 Ministry of Justice

なぜ「唐獅子に牡丹」なのか？

　襖絵、着物、刺青、花札などには昔から意味のある図像が使われることが多い。「唐獅子に牡丹」の組み合わせもその一つ。獅子(ライオン)は百獣の王であり、牡丹は百花の王である。伝説では強い獅子でも体内に巣食う虫に体力を奪われることがある。「獅子身中の虫」は権力者が味方の中に反逆者を抱え込むことだ。その虫を殺すのに最適なのが、夜、牡丹から滴る花の露だという。王者としての勇壮さや意気軒昂ぶりを示す図柄である。

　似たような組み合わせに「竹林の虎」がある。強い獣である虎も象は苦手。竹林に身を潜めれば象から身を守ることができる。

雨の中、柳の下にたたずむ男性

　日本の伝統的なカードゲームである花札は4枚×12ヵ月分の計48枚でひと組だが、一枚だけ人物の描かれた札がある。柳の木の傍で傘をさして立っている。よく見ると柳の枝に向かって蛙が飛びつこうとしている。この人物は小野道風(894–968年)という実在の人物。平安時代の貴族だが書家として有名な人。彼が書道に上達したのは、蛙が柳の枝に飛びつこうと何度も失敗するのだが、ついに飛びつけたのに感動し、努力を重ねようと発奮したからだというエピソードがある。

Why are Chinese lions paired with peonies?

There are many iconographic images with a particular meaning that have traditionally been used on painted *fusuma* doors, kimono, tattoos, and Japanese *hanafuda* playing cards, among other things. The pairing of a Chinese lion with peonies is one of these. The lion is the king of beasts, and the peony is the king of flowers. According to legend, even the strong lion was robbed of its strength by a worm it gave shelter to in its body, and the saying, "The worm in the lion's body" refers to a person in power embracing a traitor amongst his friends. It is said that the best means to kill the worm is with drops of the night dew from a peony blossom. The design shows the bravery and invincibility of a ruler.

A similar pairing is that of a tiger in a bamboo thicket. Even a beast so strong as a tiger is afraid of elephants, and so it hides in a bamboo thicket. If it manages to conceal itself, it will be saved from the elephant.

☐ 図像 iconographic image
☐ 唐獅子 Chinese lion
☐ 牡丹 peony
☐ 百獣の王 king of beasts
☐ 伝説 legend
☐ 虫 worm
☐ 奪われる be robbed
☐ 反逆者 traitor
☐ 抱え込む embrace
☐ 露 dew
☐ 勇壮さ bravery
☐ 意気軒昂 invincibility
☐ 組み合わせ pairing
☐ 竹林 bamboo thicket
☐ 象 elephant

A man standing beneath a willow tree in the rain

In the traditional *hanafuda* card game, there are twelve suits, one for each month, with four cards in each, giving a total pack of forty-eight cards, but there is just one card with the figure of a person on it. He is standing beside a willow tree holding up an umbrella, and if you look closely, you will also see a frog jumping towards one of the willow branches. This is a real person by the name of Ono no Tōfū (894–968), who was a noble at the Heian court, but is famous for his calligraphy. It is said that he was so impressed at seeing the frog repeatedly trying to jump onto the willow branch and failing many times before finally succeeding that he was inspired to redouble his own efforts to refine his skill in calligraphy.

☐ 柳 willow
☐ 傘 umbrella
☐ 貴族 noble
☐ 書道 calligraphy
☐ 何度も repeatedly
☐ 努力を重ねる redouble one's own efforts
☐ 発奮する be inspired to

4.レジャー

33

日本（にほん）の国技（こくぎ）「相撲（すもう）」は神事（しんじ）の一種（いっしゅ）

　相撲（すもう）は古（ふる）くから行（おこな）われた格闘技（かくとうぎ）で、古墳（こふん）から出土（しゅつど）する埴輪（はにわ）にも「力士（りきし）」（相撲取（すもうと）り）をかたどったものがあるという。平安時代（へいあんじだい）には宮中（きゅうちゅう）で行（おこな）われる神事（しんじ）の一（ひと）つでもあった。また江戸時代（えどじだい）には大名（だいみょう）が人気力士（にんきりきし）の後援者（こうえんしゃ）になり、興行（こうぎょう）としても盛（さか）んになる。当時（とうじ）の相撲場所（すもうばしょ）は年（ねん）に２回（かい）、野外（やがい）で晴天（せいてん）の日（ひ）に10日間（とおかかん）開催（かいさい）された。

　相撲（すもう）の所作（しょさ）は神事（しんじ）にもとづいている。土俵（どひょう）に清（きよ）めの塩（しお）を撒（ま）いたり、「四股（しこ）」を踏（ふ）んで神霊（しんれい）を呼（よ）び出（だ）し、しゃがんで胸（むね）を張（は）る「蹲踞（そんきょ）」の姿勢（しせい）から両手（りょうて）を左右（さゆう）に開（ひら）いて武器（ぶき）を隠（かく）し持（も）たないことを見（み）せる……など。土俵（どひょう）自体（じたい）が神聖（しんせい）な場所（ばしょ）であるし、屋根（やね）を持（も）つ土俵（どひょう）では東西南北（とうざいなんぼく）の柱（はしら）に青（あお）・白（しろ）・朱（しゅ）・黒（くろ）の布（ぬの）が巻（ま）かれる。これは中国伝来（ちゅうごくでんらい）の「四神相応（しじんそうおう）」の思想（しそう）にもとづくもので、「青（あお）＝青龍（せいりゅう）＝春（はる）＝東（ひがし）」「白（しろ）＝白虎（びゃっこ）＝秋（あき）＝西（にし）」「朱（しゅ）＝朱雀（すざく）＝夏（なつ）＝南（みなみ）」「黒（くろ）＝玄武（げんぶ）(亀（かめ）)＝冬（ふゆ）＝北（きた）」をそれぞれ意味（いみ）している。

　国技館（こくぎかん）は観客（かんきゃく）のために柱（はしら）がなく、屋根（やね）の下（した）につけた房（ふさ）の色（いろ）で「四神（しじん）」を表現（ひょうげん）している。

4. Leisure

Japan's national sport, Sumo, is a kind of Shinto ritual

Sumo is a combat sport that has been practiced since ancient times, and it is said that some of the *haniwa* figures excavated from burial mounds are modeled after sumo wrestlers. It was also one of the rituals held at the Imperial Court in Heian times. Much later, in the Edo period, it flourished as popular entertainment as daimyo became patrons of popular wrestlers. At that time sumo tournaments were held twice a year in the open air for ten days during fine weather.

Sumo customs are based on ritual. Wrestlers scatter purifying salt in the ring, stamp the ground in the ring to summon the gods, and at the beginning of the bout squat with their chests thrust out and their arms open wide to show that they are unarmed. The ring itself is a sacred space, and under the covered rings the pillars to the east, west, south and north are adorned with green, white, red, and black cloths. This based on the philosophy of the Chinese Taoist ideal topography of green=green dragon=spring=east, white=white tiger=autumn=west, red=red bird=summer= south, and black=black tortoise=winter=north.

In the Kokugikan stadium the pillars are omitted for the sake of the audience, but four tassels, one of each color, hang from the roof in their place.

□格闘技 combat sport
□古墳 burial mound
□出土する be excavated
□力士 sumo wrestler
□宮中 Imperial court
□神事 ritual
□後援者 patron
□興行 entertainment
□盛んになる flourish
□相撲場所 sumo tournament
□野外で in the open air
□清めの塩 purifying salt
□撒く scatter
□四股を踏む stamp the ground
□呼び出す summon
□柱 pillar
□思想 philosophy
□観客 audience
□房 tassel

四股(左)と蹲踞(右)の姿勢
Shiko (Left) and *Sonkyo* (Right) Poses

身近な娯楽は「寄席」と「芝居」

　人を笑わせたり泣かせたりする話芸の「落語」は江戸の元禄時代（1688–1704年）に生まれたとされる。最初は道端や寺の境内あるいは個人の家で行っていたのが、人気の高まりとともに常設の小屋である「寄席」で行うようになった。この「寄席」には落語のほかにも、主に歴史ものや教訓ものの話をする「講談」専門のがあったり、手品芸、女性が人形浄瑠璃を語る「女義太夫」を披露するものなどがあった。

　人気の高さでは歌舞伎や狂言を演ずる芝居小屋もひけをとらなかった。こちらも人気の高まりとともに設備にも凝るようになり、役者が客席から舞台に歩ける「花道」や、「桟敷」「せり」「どんでん」などの仕掛けも作られるようになった。

　寄席や芝居の人気が過熱してくると幕府は何度も取締りを行ったが、効果は少なかった。

高級なファンに支えられた能楽

　今日、その芸術性を国際的にも高く評価されている能楽は、歴史的には何度も浮き沈みを繰り返し、何度も廃れかけた。そのつど有力な大名や明治政府の大臣などが後援してきた。舞によって表現される劇を楽しむだけでなく、演目の筋やせりふを歌いこむ「謡曲」のファンも多い。

Yose and *shibai*: two popular amusements

The art of storytelling called *rakugo*, which can move the audience to both laughter and tears, is thought to have started during the Genroku era (1688–1704) of the Edo period. At first it was held on the roadside or in temple grounds, or in individual residences, but as it became more popular it came to be held in permanent halls called *yose*. In addition to *rakugo*, these halls were used for the *kōdan* storytellers specializing in history or moral teachings, as well as magic shows, and *jōruri* puppet shows narrated by women.

Equally popular were the *shibai* playhouses where *kabuki* and the comic *kyōgen* skits were performed. These too acquired their own facilities as their popularity grew, and developed features such as the *hanamichi* walkway where the actors would walk from the audience to the stage, and the tiered seating, stage elevators and traps, and stage sets that can be flipped over to reveal a new scene.

The *bakufu* government often cracked down on the *yose* and *shibai* as their popularity reached fever pitch, without much success.

☐ 話芸 art of storytelling

☐ 道端 roadside

☐ 寺の境内 temple ground

☐ 個人の家 individual residence

☐ 常設の permanent

☐ 教訓もの moral teaching

☐ 手品芸 magic show

☐ 桟敷 tiered seating

☐ せり stage elevator

☐ どんでん traps, and stage sets that can be flipped over to reveal a new scene

☐ 過熱する reach fever pitch

☐ 取締る crack down

The Noh theater supported by high-class fans

The Noh theater has today garnered international acclaim for its artistry, but historically it has been through many ups and downs. Each time it was on the verge of becoming obsolete, however, a powerful *daimyo* or Meiji era minister of state would step in to support it. Its many fans enjoy not just the drama it portrays through dance, but the plays themselves and the chanted lines known as *yōkyoku*.

☐ 芸術性 artistry

☐ 評価 acclaim

☐ 能楽 Noh theater

☐ 浮き沈み up and down

☐ 廃れる obsolete

☐ 後援 support

☐ 演目 play

季節ごとの賑わいを見せる行楽

　日本人は、先に書いた「お花見」のように、四季折々の変化を娯楽として楽しんできた。春には桜の「花見」があり、初夏には**遠浅の海岸**で貝を拾う「潮干狩り」、夏には江戸・両国の「川開き」と盛大な**花火見物**。「川開き」には、船に乗って川を上り下りし、飲食も楽しむ川遊びが解禁される。夏には「七夕」「盆踊り」「**蛍狩り**」などもある。秋には菊で作った人形などを楽しむ催しに出かけたり、**紅葉の名所**に出かける「紅葉狩り」をした。冬でさえ、**粋人**たちは「雪見」の酒を楽しんだ。

Lively seasonal outings

As I already mentioned under *ohanami* blossom viewing, Japanese people have always enjoyed particular seasonal entertainments throughout the year. In spring there was cherry blossom viewing, in early summer people gathered shellfish on the beach at low tide, a practice called *shiohigari*, and at the height of summer, there were the magnificent fireworks display and the *kawabiraki*, or "river opening" held in Ryōgoku in Edo. This was a festival to mark the beginning of the boating season, during which people could enjoy wining and dining on pleasure trips up and down the river. Summer was also the season for the *tanabata* star festival, the *bon-odori* dance for the Obon festival, and catching fireflies. In autumn people enjoyed displays of dolls made out chrysanthemums and going to famous spots to enjoy the autumn colors. Even in winter, people with refined tastes would enjoy drinking sake while gazing out at a snowy landscape.

☐ 花見 (cherry) blossom viewing

☐ 娯楽 entertainment

☐ 遠浅の海岸 beach at low tide

☐ 貝 shellfish

☐ 花火 firework

☐ 蛍狩り catching fireflies

☐ 紅葉 autumn colors

☐ 粋人 people with refined tastes

☐ 雪見 gazing out at a snowy landscape

5. 趣味

34

役に立たないことに夢中になる「道楽」

　日本語の「**道楽**」という言葉には少し**否定的**あるいは**自嘲的**なニュアンスがある。**女性との浮気に夢中になれば**「**女道楽**」、**釣りならば**「**釣り道楽**」、芝居に夢中になれば「**芝居道楽**」、衣装や着こなしに凝れば「**着道楽**」、そして継承すべき**家業**にも勉学にも役立たないことに夢中になって**遺産を食い潰す子供を**「**道楽息子**」などといった具合。

　こういう**無益な**ことへののめりこみを**戒める言葉**として「**道楽**もほどほどに」という。本来、この言葉は、**修行**の末に悟りを開くことの楽しみをさす仏教用語だった。同じような言葉に「**～三昧**」というのがあり、道楽のし放題を「**道楽三昧**」、贅沢のし放題なら「**贅沢三昧**」といった。この言葉ももとは仏教用語で、精神がもっとも集中している状態のことだった。

5. Hobbies

Getting into useless pastimes

The Japanese word *dōraku*, which means pastime, has a nuance of denial, or of self-deprecation. Getting into womanizing is called *onna-dōraku,* fishing is *tsuri-dōraku,* being obsessed with the theater is *shibai-dōraku,* and being into clothes and style is *ki-dōraku,* while an heir to the family business who plays around and fritters away his inheritance without studying or doing anything useful is called a *dōraku-musuko.*

The phrase *Dōraku mo hodohodo ni* ("Pastimes in moderation too") serves as a warning against getting too swept away in such futile pursuits. It was originally a Buddhist word indicating the enjoyment of attaining enlightenment following ascetic training. *Zanmai* is another Buddhist word referring to a state of perfect spiritual concentration. These days, adding *zanmai* to a word enhances the meaning, so that *dōraku-zanmai* means "a life of pleasure and gaiety," while *zeitaku-zanmai* means "luxury and extravagance."

☐ 道楽 pastime
☐ 否定的 denial
☐ 自嘲的 self-deprecation
☐ 女性との浮気 womanizing
☐ 夢中になる get into, be obsessed with
☐ 釣り fishing
☐ 家業 family business
☐ 遺産を食い潰す fritter away one's inheritance
☐ 無益な futile
☐ 戒める言葉 warning
☐ 修行 ascetic training
☐ 贅沢三昧 luxury and extravagance

何事も「道」にしたがる日本人

　日本人は一面では、生真面目にものごとに取り組むところがある。こういう人は趣味の世界でも高い精神性を求めようとする。「華道」「茶道」「香道」などのように、所作を洗練させ、奥深い精神性を伴う体系にし、いつのまにか日本文化を代表するものに仕立てた。

　「柔道」「剣道」「空手道」など武術の世界でも「道」を追求する姿勢が見られ、「武士道」という考え方も生まれた。これらは趣味というよりも、日々の鍛錬であり、生き方であり、哲学や美学に通じているといえる。古代中国の思想家である老子が説いた「道」の教えは、宇宙の真理・真相に迫る道だったが、そうした影響があるのかもしれない。

　永遠に続く奥深い真理への道を歩もうとする精神的な傾向は、過去の話ではない。現代人も職場においては品質とサービス向上のための「カイゼン」を続けているし、大衆文化の世界でも「ラーメン道」とか「マンガ道」を提唱している人たちもいる。こうした分野からも将来の、世界が感心するような日本文化が生まれるのかもしれない。

Japanese people make everything into a "way"

Many Japanese people throw themselves into pursuits with extreme earnestness, and such people seek a high level of spirituality even in their hobbies. In *kadō*, the way of flower arranging, *chadō*, the way of tea, *kōdō*, the way of incense, and others, the skills were polished and made into a profoundly spiritual practice, and in no time these pastimes ended up being representative of Japanese culture.

This attitude of pursuing a "way" (*michi*, or *dō*) can also be seen in the martial arts, with jūdō, kendō, karate-dō and so forth, and led to the way of thinking called *bushidō*, or the way of the warrior. These have become more than hobbies, and are in fact a way of life and daily training, with their own philosophy and aesthetic. They have also probably been influenced by the teachings of Lao-zi, who held that the "way" approached the ultimate truth of the universe.

The trend to follow the spiritual way to this profound and eternal truth is not something of the past. People today, too, follow the *kaizen* philosophy of continual improvement in service and quality in business, and even in popular culture there are people who advocate the "way of ramen," and the "way of manga." Maybe these will lead to some future Japanese culture that will impress the world.

☐ 生真面目に with extreme earnestness
☐ 取り組む pursue
☐ 精神性 spirituality
☐ 華道 flower arranging
☐ 茶道 way of tea
☐ 香道 way of incense
☐ 奥深い profoundly
☐ 代表 representative
☐ 武術 martial arts
☐ 追求する pursue
☐ 趣味 hobby
☐ 鍛錬 training
☐ 哲学 philosophy
☐ 美学 aesthetic
☐ 宇宙の真理・真相 ultimate truth of the universe
☐ 奥深い profound
☐ 品質 quality
☐ 大衆文化 popular culture
☐ 提唱する advocate

玄関　entrance
げんかん

ガラガラという音を立てる引き戸を開けて入
おと　た　ひ　ど　あ　はい
る。履き物を脱いで、一段高い板張りの「あがり
は　もの　ぬ　いちだんたか　いたば
口」に上がる。脱いだ履き物は、つま先を入口の
ぐち　あ　ぬ　は　もの　さき　いりぐち
方に向けて揃え直すのが礼儀。
ほう　む　そろ　なお　れいぎ

You enter through a sliding door that clatters
as you open it. You take off your footwear and
step up on to the raised wooden floor called the
agariguchi. It is good manners to rearrange your
shoes so the toes are pointing towards the door.

和室　Japanese-style rooms
わしつ

畳 敷きの部屋で、その数によって6畳間、8畳間などと呼ばれる。古い日本家屋の
たたみじ　　へや　　　　かず　　　　じょうま　じょうま　　　　よ　　　ふる　にほんかおく
場合は、必要に応じて各部屋を仕切る襖を取り外すと、広い部屋になるという工夫
ばあい　ひつよう　おう　かくへや　しき　ふすま　と　はず　　ひろ　へや　　　　　くふう
がこらされている。

Rooms are laid with *tatami* mats, the number of which determine the room size of the
room, as in 6-mat rooms, 8-mat rooms and
so forth. Old Japanese houses were devised
so that sliding doors could be removed to
create larger rooms as necessary.

和式トイレ　Japanese-style toilets

便器に腰を掛ける欧米式と違い、和式は入口を
背にして便器にまたがり用を足す。男性の小用
は立ったまま行う。欧米式に慣れた人には、
ちょっとしたカルチャーショックだ。

Unlike Western toilets, on which you sit over the
bowl, in Japanese toilets you squat over the bowl
with your back to the door. Men can stand over
them to urinate. For people used to Western-style
toilets, they can come as a bit of a shock.

床の間　alcove

床を一段高くして置物や花瓶を置き、壁に書画などを掛ける。茶室にもみられるも
ので、新しい日本家屋の和室の一室は必ず床の間つきになっている。

The *tokonoma* is an alcove slightly raised
from floor level in which an ornament
or flower vase is placed, with a painting
or piece of calligraphy hung on the wall.
They can be seen in tearooms, and even a
Japanese-style room in a new house will
have a *tokonoma*.

風呂　bath

古い日本家屋は風呂も木製だったが、現在はめっきり見かけなくなった。しかし、入浴法は昔のままで、身体を洗う時は浴槽から出て洗うのが日本流である。

In old Japanese houses even the bath was made of wood, but nowadays these have all but disappeared. However, the way of bathing remains unchanged, and you should never wash yourself while in the tub.

障子　paper screen

木組みをほどこした戸に和紙を張ったもので、自然の採光や室内の保温に適している。日本家屋ならではの独特の工夫である。

These are screens made of a wooden frame onto which *washi* paper is pasted, and they are good for allowing in natural light and keeping the room warm. They are unique to Japanese houses.

雨戸　shutter

日中は収納しておいて、夜は「戸袋」から引き出して使う。雨の日に閉めたことから「雨戸」というが、現在は防犯やプライバシーを守ることが主な役目になっている。

These are shutters that are opened during the day and stored away in built-in compartments, and pulled closed to cover windows at night. They are called *amado*, or "rain doors," since they used to be kept closed on rainy days, but now their main function is to prevent burglaries and maintain privacy.

押入れ　cupboard

寝具や日常使わないものの保管場所として、和室に付設されている。昔の日本の子供は、親に叱られると、ここに逃げ込んだものだ。

These are the large built-in cupboards in Japanese-style rooms where bedding and items not in daily use are stored. In the past children used to hide in them when scolded by their parents.

こたつ　heated table

家族全員がこたつに入って暖をとるのが、日本の冬の当たり前の家庭風景だった。家庭崩壊は、暖房の発達でこたつが不要になったことと無縁ではないのかもしれない。

The whole family gathered around a warm *kotatsu*—a low table heated from below and covered by a quilt—used to be a typical winter scene in Japan. Family breakdown is perhaps not unrelated to the fact that the *kotatsu* has largely been replaced by central heating.

寝具　Bedding

和室に布団を敷いて寝るのが、昔の日本人の一般的風習だった。夜になると、和室は寝室に早変わりする。

This is the bedding used in a Japanese-style room. All Japanese people used to sleep on a *futon* mattress laid out on the *tatami*. At night, the living room was thus quickly converted into a bedroom.

仏壇 Buddhist altar

先祖の位牌を祀った仏壇に向かって手を合わせ、一日のスタートをする日本人が多い。

Even today, many people start the day by putting their hands together in prayer before the family's Buddhist altar containing the ancestral memorial tablet.

神棚 Shintō altar

商売をしている家、農家、漁師の家などは、たいがい神様を祀る神棚を設けている。

Most households involved in trades such as shopkeeping, farming, or fishing keep a shrine dedicated to their patron god.

Read Real NIHONGO

ニッポンのしきたり
Customs of Japan

2023年11月4日　第1刷発行

著　者　土屋　晴仁

発行者　浦　　晋亮

発行所　IBCパブリッシング株式会社
　　　　〒162-0804 東京都新宿区中里町29番3号　菱秀神楽坂ビル
　　　　Tel. 03-3513-4511　Fax. 03-3513-4512
　　　　www.ibcpub.co.jp

印刷所　株式会社シナノパブリッシングプレス

ISBN978-4-7946-0787-4